18th-century festive
headdress for a
married woman

Flag of the Russian Soviet Federal
Socialist Republic from 1920 to 1954

Icon of St. Nicholas

Silver samovar for
making tea

Soviet leader
Joseph Stalin

Yury Dolgoruky,
founder of Moscow

EYEWITNESS BOOKS

RUSSIA

Wooden coat of arms
for Russia, 1882

Hat pin of
Cossack leader
Bodgdan
Khmelnitsky

series: Eyewitness Books

Written by
KATHLEEN BERTON MURRELL

Photographed by
ANDY CRAWFORD

Civil War
saber owned
by General
Tulenov

Red Army *shlam* hat

Brightly painted
19th-century
cotton spinner

ALFRED A. KNOPF • NEW YORK

Strings of
dried mushrooms

A DORLING KINDERSLEY BOOK

Project editor Melanie Halton
Art editor Vicky Wharton
Senior managing editor Gillian Denton
Senior managing art editor Julia Harris
Production Lisa Moss
Picture research Monica Allende
DTP designer Nicola Studdart

This is a Borzoi Book published by Alfred A. Knopf, Inc.

This Eyewitness ® Guide has been conceived by
Dorling Kindersley Limited and Editions Gallimard.

First American edition, 1998

http://www.randomhouse.com/

Printed in Singapore
0 9 8 7 6 5 4 3 2 1

Library of Congress Cataloging-in-Publication Data
Murrell, Kathleen Berton.
Russia / Kathleen Berton Murrell.
p. cm. – (Eyewitness books ; v. 74)
Includes index.
Summary: An overview of the land, people, history, and
culture of Russia from its earliest days to the present.
ISBN 0-679-89118-8 (trade). – ISBN 0-679-99118-2 (lib. bdg.)
1. Russia – History – Juvenile lietrature. 2. Soviet Union –
History – Juvenile literature 3. Russia (Federation) – Histroy
– 1991 – Juvenile literature.
[1. Russia – History. 2. Soviet Union – History. 3. Russia
(Federation) History.]
I. Title.
DK41.M965 1998
947 – dc21
97-38878

Color reproduction by
Colourscan, Singapore
Printed in Singapore by Toppan

Alexander Pushkin's
silver tea strainer

16th–17th
century Russian
pole ax

Nikolai Gogol's
feather quill

Wooden
gingerbread
mold

Catherine the
Great's ivory
hunting gun

Cross-country
skis and poles

Early 19th-century Russian ice skates

Contents

Vladimir Lenin's funeral train

Early Russia

MODERN RUSSIANS ORIGINATE from the eastern Slavs who settled in the steppelands of European Russia in the 6th century. In the 9th century Vikings, *Varangians*, sailed from the Baltic Sea along the Dnieper River to establish the trade route from Scandinavia to Byzantium. One of their chieftains, Rurik, founded the first dynasty of Russian princes, and his successor, Oleg, established Kievan Rus, the first Russian state. Catastrophe struck in 1237 when Tatar (Mongol) forces raided many Russian cities, which then remained under Tatar rule for 200 years. Russia was split into many small principalities, one of which, Moscow, gradually gained power and broke the Tatar control.

LARGE AND WEALTHY
Prince Oleg founded Kievan Rus in the 9th century. For 400 years it was one of the largest and richest states in Europe under great rulers such as Vladimir I, Yaroslav the Wise, and Vladimir Monomakh. But in 1237 Kiev, weakened by internal feuding, was destroyed by the Mongol forces (Golden Horde) of Batu, grandson of Genghis Khan.

Kievan 12th-century gold enamel pendants were used to adorn headdresses

RURIK THE VIKING CHIEFTAIN
The *Varangians* were Norsemen, or Vikings, who in the 9th century penetrated from the Baltic Sea into the land of the eastern Slavs, attracted by the trade route between Scandinavia and Greek Byzantium. The Slavs, plagued by enemies and internal feuds, invited the *Varangians* to come and rule over them. One of the *Varangian* chieftains, Rurik, took up the challenge to become prince of Novgorod in 862. The few Norsemen were soon absorbed by the Slavs and the House of Rurik reigned until the end of the 16th century.

FROM KIEV TO MUSCOVY
At its peak, in 1054, the Kievan state stretched from the Black Sea to the Baltic Sea, and north to Lake Onega. After the decline of Kiev, Russia's center moved northeast, first to Vladimir and then to Moscow, capital of the principality of Muscovy. Muscovy included lands as far north as the White Sea and east beyond the Volga, to western Siberia.

RULER OF THE MONGOLS
From his base in Asia, the remarkable Mongol leader Genghis Khan conquered China, northern India, what is now Pakistan, and Central Asia. Later, in 1222, he swept into southern Russia with his brilliant mounted troops, plundering the land between the Volga and Dnieper rivers. His grandson, Batu, completed the domination of Russia in 1237, taking most of Kievan Rus and the newer towns of Vladimir and Suzdal before riding west to conquer Hungary and Poland.

Armor for a
14th–15th century
Mongol warrior

*These flexible
plates protect the
neck and allow
easy movement*

THE GOLDEN HORDE
The followers of Genghis Khan and his grandson,
Batu, were skilled horsemen and archers well
protected by impressive armor. Batu established
the headquarters of his state, the Golden Horde,
at Sarai at the mouth of the Volga. The Mongol
overlords did not attempt to colonize the Russian
principalities but kept control with frequent raids
and by demanding heavy annual payments.
Although the Orthodox Church was tolerated
by the Mongols, their 200-year rule severely
retarded the development of Russian
cultural and social life.

*Leather straps
fasten the upper
part of the suit*

FIGHTING THE TATARS
Moscow gradually became the center of
opposition to the Tatars (Mongols). In
1380 the Moscow prince Dmitry defeated
the Tatars on the River Don, and in 1480
another Moscow prince, Ivan III, tore up
the document demanding tributes. But it
was not until the 16th century that Russian
forces, under Ivan the Terrible, succeeded
in recapturing land from the Tatars.

*Ribbon of
St. Andrew was
the highest award
in tsarist Russia*

*Scepter that was
originally held
by the eagle on
this wooden coat
of arms of 1882
has long since
disappeared*

*Double-headed
eagle holds orb,
a symbol of
state power*

COAT OF ARMS
The double-headed eagle, a
popular symbol of state power
in Byzantium and Europe, was
also adopted in 15th-century Muscovy,
together with the figure of St. George
slaying a dragon. In 1672 the state coat of
arms was declared to be the double-headed
eagle wearing three crowns and holding
the orb and scepter, with St. George on a
shield at the center, surrounded by the
arms of major towns and Siberia. Later the
arms of Finland, Poland, Georgia, and
Taurida (Crimea) were added, together
with the ribbon of St. Andrew.

*St. George
and the dragon*

*The flexible armor
came below the knee
for maximum
protection*

*Mongols relied
on their accuracy
with bow and
arrow to bring
down the enemy*

*Mongol warriors
slashed with the sword
during close encounters*

A varied land

RUSSIA IS THE LARGEST country in the world, straddling the two continents of Europe and Asia and crossing 11 time zones. Its three geographical regions are European Russia in the west, up to the low-lying Ural Mountains; the huge, flat expanse of Siberia; and the mountainous far eastern region. The climate is extreme – average temperatures range from -4°F (-20°C) in winter to 68°F (+20°C) in summer. Russia's mighty rivers include the Volga, Europe's longest river, and the Yenisei in Siberia. Huge Lake Baikal in eastern Siberia is the deepest in the world and contains one fifth of the world's fresh water. Russia's rich variety of animal life includes tigers, reindeer, moose, sable, walrus, and the unique Baikal seal.

Reins attached to these notches are used to steer the sleigh

SOLITARY TIGER
The magnificent Siberian tiger, the largest tiger in the world, lives in solitude in the forests and mountains of the far eastern Ussuri region. Although the number of Siberian tigers fell disastrously to about 20 in the 1940s, a policy of protection has ensured their survival. By the mid-1990s, about 300 were known to exist.

SYMBOL OF A NATION
The common brown bear, one of the national symbols of Russia, lives in the mountains and forests of the entire country from Europe to Siberia and the mountains of the Ussuri region, in the far east. Such large creatures can sustain themselves in semihibernation throughout the winter on the fruits and berries of the forests; on fish; and even on deer which they can bring down by covering short distances at enormous speed.

Traditionally drawn by three horses, a Russian sleigh is often called a troika, from the Russian for "three"

Curved front shields passengers from spray kicked up by the horses

Animal furs make snug blankets for passengers

IN A COLD CLIMATE
Surprisingly, Russia's severe climate has not impeded winter travel, for roads of packed snow are smoother than the ruts of summer or the muddy tracks of spring and autumn. Horse-drawn sleighs, such as this one, can travel rapidly over snowy highways while passengers recline snugly under the furs. In the past, when sleighs traveled long distances, horses were changed at government post stations, placed at regular intervals along the main routes. Although most sleighs have now been replaced by cars and trucks, they are still used in some rural areas.

Step enables passengers to climb into and out of the sleigh easily

TUNDRA SUMMER
In June and July the warm sun thaws the Arctic soil a few inches down to the permafrost, permanently frozen earth over 0.62 miles (1 km) thick. During this time, the normally bleak landscape is briefly transformed by brightly colored flowers and green grasses.

SIBERIAN SURVIVAL
This ivory carving shows how the reindeer makes it possible for people to live in the isolated parts of northern Siberia. Indigenous (native) peoples, such as the Chukchi, rely on domesticated reindeer herds to provide transportation, meat, milk, and hides for clothing and tents.

VEGETATION ZONES
Russia can be divided into broad horizontal bands of vegetation: the treeless tundra in the north, which widens eastward to include the far eastern region; the taiga, the great forests that dominate most of Russia; and the steppes, or meadowlands, in the south.

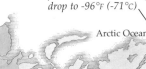

In Verkhoyansk, the coldest inhabited place in the world, temperatures can drop to -96°F (-71°C)

Arctic Ocean

•Moscow

Don

Volga

Ural Mountains

Yenisei

Ob

Lena

Kamchatka Peninsula

Siberia

Russian Federation

Lake Baikal

Vladivostok

☐ Steppe
☐ Taiga
☐ Tundra

TAIGA FORESTS
The great taiga forests of larch, pine, spruce, birch, and aspen account for over half of the world's resources of softwood and provide habitats for many of Russia's wide variety of animal species.

GRASSY PLAINS
Steppes, or treeless grasslands, are distinguished by a thick layer of extremely fertile black earth that is ideal for agriculture. The steppes are found in the southern parts of European Russia and Siberia.

Cushioned backrest provides comfort on long journeys

Handle is gripped by the coachman when the sleigh is in motion

Coachman sits on leather stool during journey

Coat of arms indicates that this sleigh belonged to an important family

FRIEND OR FOE?
The villain of Russian fairy tales, the large gray wolf is now found only in the wilds of Siberia and the remoter areas of European Russia. With its thick fur, which whitens the farther north it travels, it adapts admirably to life in a cold climate. Its poor reputation is undeserved, for although it will kill sheep and farm animals when in desperate hunger, attacks on human beings are very rare.

These shoe-shaped leather footrests protect the coachman's feet from the harsh elements

Distinctive black-and-white wing markings

Metal blades stabilize the sleigh as it glides over ice

RED-BREASTED GOOSE
Black, white, and chestnut red, these most vivid of all geese breed in the far northern reaches of Siberia, bordering on the Arctic Ocean. These beautiful birds are living proof that the huge, almost uninhabited regions of Russia's cold north can support a colorful variety of life during the warmer months of the year, June to August. But the number of breeding pairs has declined by over two thirds in the past century, mostly because of indiscriminate hunting.

Peoples of Russia

Before the Revolution, Russia was a truly multiethnic empire, which included Ukrainians and Belorussians; Kazakhs and other peoples of Central Asia; Georgians, Armenians, and Azerbaijanis in the Caucasus region; Lithuanians, Latvians, and Estonians in the north; Tatars; Germans; and many others. Even present-day Russia, which is much smaller, has over 100 nationalities among its 150 million people. But ethnically "Russian" Russians are the vast majority, at 82 percent of the population. Just over half the Soviet Union's people were Russian, and in the Russian empire Russians were a minority.

Soft swansdown pom-pom

COSSACKS
Russians largely made up the Cossack (p. 23) self-governing communities in the Kuban, Astrakhan, and Orenburg provinces in the south. However, some Cossack settlements were not Russian but Kalmyk and Buryat (Mongol peoples), Bashkir (Turkic-speaking), and Tungus (native Siberian).

KOKOSHNIK
Red velvet hats with gold embroidery, like this one, were Russian women's everyday wear for centuries. All but the highest nobility wore the *kokoshnik*.

FAMILY HEIRLOOM
This festive 19th-century outfit with its delightful pom-pom hat comes from the Ryazan area, south of Moscow. The owner would have made the blouse, skirt, apron, and sleeveless jacket herself. She would have spun the linen thread from flax, then woven the material and sewn the clothes together. Finally she would have done all the embroidery and crochetwork. Such a fine outfit would have been handed down within the family.

Ryazan designs are typically geometric

Apron displays fine crochetwork

NATIONAL DRESS
Along with the *kokoshnik*, Russian peasant and servant women all over the country wore a sleeveless dress (*sarafan*) until the 20th century. The decoration and color of the *sarafan* differed greatly from district to district.

REPUBLIC OF TATARSTAN

Turkic-speaking Tatars form about 4 percent of the population of Russia – about 6 million people. Most live in the Republic of Tatarstan within the Russian Federation. They are descendants of the Golden Horde (p. 11) and many of them are Muslims. In 1994 Tatarstan signed a treaty giving it special rights within the Federation.

Hooded costume of Tatar women reflects the now rare custom of veil wearing

Hood prevents loss of body heat and keeps head and ears warm in sub-zero temperatures

Tungus nomad

Tungus town dweller

Men of Tobolsk

NATIVES OF SIBERIA

Today Russians greatly outnumber the many small groups of indigenous (native) Siberian peoples. The two native Siberians (above right) are from the Tobolsk area, west of the Urals. Those on the left are Tungus from the Amur district on the border of China. The one in the long fur-lined coat is a town dweller and next to him is a nomad, who lives with his reindeer herds.

Mittens are sewn into the sleeves to keep out biting winds

THE NORTHERN PEOPLE

This warm coat comes from the Nganasan people, the most northerly inhabitants of Russia, whose way of life resembles that of the Inuit. There are only a few thousand Nganasan; they belong to the Samoyed-Nenets group and live on the Taimyr Peninsula in northern Siberia. They lived traditionally as nomadic hunters, reindeer herders, and fishermen, although in the Soviet period many were forced to settle on collective farms.

Wealth of a nation

RUSSIA HAS VAST reserves of natural resources, from timber – about one fifth of all the world's forests – to a remarkable supply of rocks and minerals. These include huge deposits of gold, diamonds, iron ore, copper, nickel, lead, and zinc. There are also large deposits of fossil fuels including coal – half the world's reserves – oil, peat, and natural gas. Fur trapping, Russia's earliest source of wealth, is still practiced. Fishing, particularly for sturgeon, is a highly developed industry, and Russia's long rivers are used to generate over 10 percent of the world's hydroelectric power.

DIAMOND DISCOVERY
Until the 19th century diamonds, such as those in the imperial crown, above, were imported from India. Russian diamonds were first discovered in 1955 in an isolated spot in north central Siberia. Within a year a new town, Mirny, had been built. It has good links by air, but the nearest railroad is over 600 miles (1,000 km) away. However, Mirny is now a town of about 40,000 people, who are mostly involved in diamond production.

Polished amber bead

Crystallized gold nugget

MINING FOR MINERALS
Iron ore and other metals are especially abundant in Siberia. The northern Siberian town of Norilsk (p. 39), beyond the Arctic Circle, was founded in the 1930s to extract rich deposits of nickel, copper, and cobalt, and now also produces gold, silver, and platinum.

ANCIENT AMBER
Amber is fossil resin – a thick, sticky substance from extinct conifers. It is found mostly along the Baltic Sea; for thousands of years, people have polished it, traded with it, and made it into jewelry. The Catherine Palace (p. 29) had a famous room lined with panels of amber.

GOLD RUSH
Russia has some of the largest gold reserves in the world. In 1838 a discovery near the Yenisei River in Siberia, followed by huge finds near the upper Lena River, started a gold rush. In 1923 another major find was made at Aldan on the upper Lena.

Russian nobleman in fur-lined coat and fur hat

Furry side flaps untie to cover ears in especially cold weather

Front flap folds down to cover forehead

FUR TRAPPING
To combat the harsh cold of winter, most Russians wear fur hats and coats with the fur on the inside. Animals are still trapped extensively in the wild, mostly by native peoples. There are also many fur farms where mink, sable, and fox are raised for their skins. But the fur of animals living in the wild is considered the best.

FUR TRADERS
Early traders from central Russia headed north and east in search of the pelts of animals from the Russian Arctic. By the 17th century fur was the most important item of foreign trade for the merchants of Moscow. The annual fur auction in St. Petersburg is still considered the most important fur market in the world.

Deep green with pale green streaks, malachite is a popular stone for carving into objects, such as this 19th-century vase from Yekaterinburg in the Urals

NATURAL GAS
The leading producer of fossil fuels, Russia has 40 percent of the world's natural gas. Deposits lie in the northern Caucasus, Siberia, and along the Arctic coast. Pipelines laid in the 1970s and 1980s, linking the Siberian gas fields with European Russia, made it much easier to export the gas to other countries. Those exports help pay for imports.

Laying pipelines in northern Russia is difficult and expensive because of permafrost (p. 11)

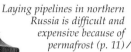

MIGHTY STURGEON
As the Volga and the Caspian Sea become polluted, the huge sturgeon that provide caviar (fish eggs), an expensive luxury dish, are becoming scarce. Nevertheless, fishing is a major industry in Russia. Russia's modern fishing fleet works both in coastal waters and out on the open seas of the Atlantic and Pacific.

Arms move up and down as if washing the bear in the tub

HYDROELECTRICITY
With its immense rivers, Russia has built many dams to generate electricity. Stalin favored huge hydroelectric projects, such as reversing the flow of rivers, but recently these have been rejected because they would damage the environment.

Traditional Russian toy carved from wood

MALACHITE
This beautiful green copper compound occurs in only four places in the world, including the Ural Mountains of Russia. In the 19th century, malachite was used to make jewelry, furniture, and beautiful objects, such as this vase, for high society. The interior walls of the Malachite Hall in the Winter Palace (p. 28), a room for ceremonial occasions, are completely lined with the bright green stone.

TIMBER
Russia has about one fifth of the world's forests and nearly half the world's softwood (pine and other conifers). Siberian forests are remote, so tree felling is concentrated nearer to markets in central Russia and the Urals. The wood is used to make paper, furniture, and village houses, and much is still used as firewood.

A life of serfdom

SERFS WERE PEASANTS bound to their landlord's estates and forced to work the land. They were virtually slaves, for they could do nothing without their lord's approval – not even marry. They could be bought and sold, exiled to Siberia, or forced to join the army. But the law forbade landlords to kill their serfs. Until the 17th century, on one day each year, serfs were allowed to move to another estate. In 1649, even this freedom was abolished. Two centuries later, in 1861, serfs were finally freed. The liberated serfs provided labor for new industry, which led to spectacular economic growth. But peasants were charged high prices for the land they believed was theirs by right; freedom brought little improvement to their lives.

THE ARISTOCRATS
Until the end of the 17th century, the aristocracy shared the same culture, language, and religion as the peasants. But as Peter the Great (pp. 20, 22) forced the nobles to shave their beards and adopt Western dress, customs, and languages, the gap between aristocrats and peasants widened immensely.

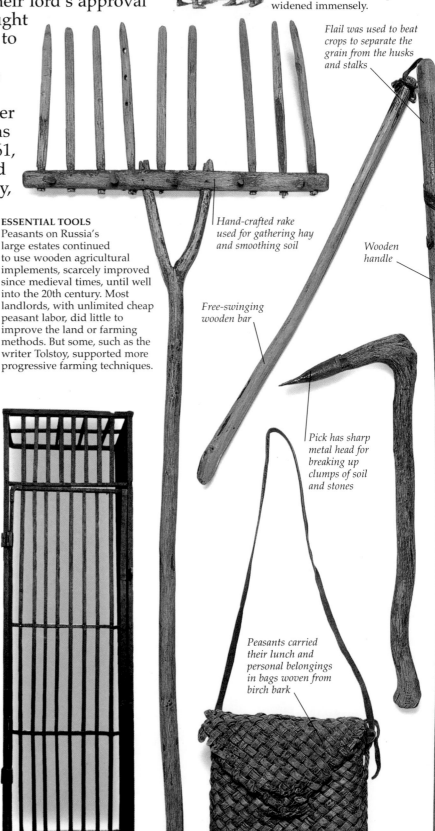

Flail was used to beat crops to separate the grain from the husks and stalks

Hand-crafted rake used for gathering hay and smoothing soil

Wooden handle

Free-swinging wooden bar

Pick has sharp metal head for breaking up clumps of soil and stones

ESSENTIAL TOOLS
Peasants on Russia's large estates continued to use wooden agricultural implements, scarcely improved since medieval times, until well into the 20th century. Most landlords, with unlimited cheap peasant labor, did little to improve the land or farming methods. But some, such as the writer Tolstoy, supported more progressive farming techniques.

Peasants carried their lunch and personal belongings in bags woven from birch bark

LOG HOUSES
Villages with identical log houses, called *izbas*, are still common all over Russia, although straw roofs are now rare. The *izba* has one large room for the extended family, dominated by a great stove that is also used as a warm sleeping bench during the long winters.

CAPTURE OF PUGACHEV
Runaway serfs fled to the borderlands in the south and became Cossacks, or free warriors, farming and organizing their communities far from the heavy hand of the tsar. In 1773 Yemelyan Pugachev, a Cossack leader, declared himself Emperor Peter III, murdered husband of Catherine the Great. Promising liberation of the serfs, he led a popular revolt of peasants of Russian and other nationalities in the Volga and Ural regions. He was at first successful, capturing Kazan and threatening Moscow, but was defeated at Tsaritsyn in August 1774. Pugachev escaped, but was captured in December and brought to Moscow in this specially built cage, and publicly tortured and executed.

PEASANT LIFE
Before the Revolution of 1917, four out of five persons in Russia were peasants. Only one fifth were literate, but they were skillful craftspeople, able to construct their own houses, spin cloth, and make all their own agricultural tools. Peasants belonged to a tight-knit village commune, or *mir*, whose elders were responsible for collecting taxes, settling disputes, and allocating land.

Loose linen blouse with lace-up collar kept peasants cool on hot summer days

Brightly colored wool skirts were spun at home

The sickle's curved blade is used to cut grass and crops, such as wheat

Female serfs often wore many layers of skirts to keep them warm in the winter

Traditional serfs' shoes, called lapti, *were hand-woven from birch bark*

FREEDOM TO THE PEOPLE
In March 1861, serfs celebrated throughout Russia as news spread of Tsar Alexander II's emancipation law. About 50 million Russian people were thus freed from near slavery. However, the former serfs were still bound to their commune and in debt for what little land they received. Many felt cheated and remained dissatisfied with their situation.

TRADITIONAL ATTIRE
Women's everyday wear was a simple blouse and skirt, or a sleeveless dress, called a *sarafan*. Men wore trousers, linen shirts, and a caftan. In summer peasants wore birch-bark shoes. In winter they put on felt boots, or *valenki*, and sheepskin overcoats with the fur on the inside, to keep themselves warm in the snow. More elaborate costumes were kept for special occasions and handed down from generation to generation.

Orthodox religion

Although many religions, including Buddhism and Islam, are found in Russia, most of the population identifies with Orthodox Christianity. Adopted from Byzantium over 1,000 years ago by Prince Vladimir, it was chosen for the splendor of its ceremonies. Rich in ritual, Orthodox services are often long, elaborate, and colorful. Priests chant and the choir sings without the accompaniment of musical instruments, because it is believed that only the human voice should be used in sacred music. Orthodoxy remained Russia's State religion until the Revolution in 1917. In the Soviet era many churches were destroyed; priests were shot or imprisoned. Since 1990, when official support was renewed, the Church has rapidly revived.

WEDDING CEREMONY
During an Orthodox marriage service, ornate crowns, like the poet Pushkin's, above, are held over the heads of the bride and groom. The couple drink wine three times from the same cup. The priest then leads the couple three times around the center of the church.

NIKON'S REFORMS
Patriarch Nikon was head of the Church from 1652 to 1658. His reforms to rituals, such as making the sign of the cross with three fingers instead of two, met with strenuous opposition from a group called the Old Believers, who separated from the Church. When Nikon tried to make the Church more powerful than the State, the tsar imprisoned him in a remote monastery.

Slanted bar on Russian Orthodox cross represents where Christ's feet were nailed

St. Nicholas, the 4th-century Byzantine bishop

Embossed metal covers this icon, revealing only the hand and face of the painted saint

SACRED PICTURES
Sculptures were discouraged by the Church for a long time because it was thought that they might become objects of worship. But icons – religious pictures painted on wooden panels – could be venerated (deeply respected) because they are not lifelike images. Icons are found not only in churches, but also in Russian homes.

MONASTERIES
Although most of the ancient monasteries were forced to close after the Bolshevik Revolution and were neglected or destroyed, many have been vigorously revived in the new Russia. The most important is the beautiful Trinity Lavra of St. Sergius, founded in the 14th century. In 1689, its enterprising monks supported Peter the Great in his struggle for the throne against his half-sister, Sophia.

Oil lamp for lighting up icons

Apostle Matthew

Apostle John

Angel tells Mary she will bear the son of God

Apostle Luke

Apostle Mark

ROYAL DOORS
The royal doors are at the center of the iconostasis – the tall wall of tiered, religious paintings that screens the altar from the rest of the church. The congregation stands throughout the service, facing the iconostasis. Only the clergy are permitted to enter through the royal doors, which are opened at certain moments during services, symbolically revealing heaven to the faithful.

CHURCH CLERGY
At the head of the Church is the patriarch. He, like all senior ranks of the Orthodox Church – the metropolitans, archbishops, bishops, and archimandrites – is drawn from the unmarried "black" clergy (monks). The more numerous priests, the "white" clergy, are normally married and often remain parish priests all their lives. Women are not permitted to enter the clergy.

Orthodox bishop

Golden chalice

Miter is a symbol of a bishop's power

Bishop's miter

Elaborately bound Book of the Gospels

HOLY BOOK
The Bible was translated into Old Church Slavonic in the 9th century by Saints Cyril and Methodius. Church Slavonic is close to the Russian language and is still used today in church services.

The stole, omoforion, is only worn by bishops

Girdle

Cuffs are laced around the wrist

The palitza, which hangs from the right hip, is worn by bishops and some senior priests

The sacchos hangs down to the mid-calf

The sacchos, or bishop's vestment, symbolizes the robe of Christ

CEREMONIAL ROBES
The robes for ceremonial occasions in the Orthodox Church are often magnificent and richly colored, like these bishop's vestments. Each item of clothing has a special religious significance. Both bishops and priests normally wear a black cassock, or robe, and a black hat (*skufya*). For services, priests have their own special vestments, many of which are similar to those of the bishop. More ornate robes are worn by bishops and priests for Easter and other important festivals.

Staff, or crosier, signifies that the bishop is a shepherd of his people

Priestly stole, epitrachelion, hangs down almost to the floor

Rule of the tsars

RUSSIA HAS KNOWN two royal dynasties: the Rurikids (c. 860–1598) and, following the Time of Troubles (c. 1605–13), the Romanovs (1613–1917). The chaotic Time of Troubles was a period of civil strife when many imposters fought for the throne, and unrest, famine, and invasion plagued the country. Russian princes adopted the title "tsar" from the Roman "Caesar" in the 15th century, as the power and prestige of Moscow grew. The title "emperor" came into use in the 18th century under Peter the Great. Tsars throughout Russian history ruled with absolute power.

THE ROMANOV DYNASTY
In 1613, 16-year-old Mikhail Romanov was elected to the throne. His family continued to rule for the next 300 years. The dynasty ended in February 1917 when Nicholas II abdicated (gave up the throne).

Gold crown studded with pearls, garnets, and turquoise

Sable-fur trimming made crown more comfortable to wear

CROWN OF KAZAN
Thought to have belonged to Ediger Mahmet, this 16th-century crown is one of the oldest in Russia. Mahmet was the last ruler of the Tatar state of Kazan. He adopted Christianity and became loyal to Ivan the Terrible.

IVAN THE TERRIBLE
Ivan IV's long rule (1533–1584) began hopefully, with new laws, territorial conquests, and commercial relations with England. After the death of his first wife, however, Ivan began a reign of terror, even murdering his own son.

Peter and Paul Fortress in St. Petersburg, painted 1723

Porcelain frame decorated with enamel on copper

BORIS GODUNOV
Unpopular Boris Godunov ruled at the end of the Rurikid dynasty. He was suspected of murdering the rightful heir, Prince Dmitry. Godunov died suddenly in 1605, resulting in a prolonged battle for a successor. The Time of Troubles had begun.

PETER THE GREAT
Peter I, who took the throne by force from his half-sister, Sophia, ruled from 1689 to 1725. The most energetic of the tsars, he founded a new capital city (pp. 28–29), established the navy (p. 22), initiated radical reforms in education and government, and was the first tsar to travel abroad.

CATHERINE II
Born a German princess, Catherine became empress of Russia in 1762 and ruled for over 30 years. Known as Catherine the Great, she was the last of four strong empresses to rule after Peter I.

DECEMBRIST REVOLT
Throughout Russian history, there were many peasant uprisings against tsarist rule. But the 1825 revolt against Nicholas I by the aristocratic Decembrists shocked the regime. With little support, the revolt soon died out. Five of the leaders were hanged and the rest condemned to hard labor in Siberia.

Executed leaders of the Decembrist Revolt

Ring made from chains that bound Decembrists in Siberia

Cupid holds the orb and scepter, which are symbols of state power

Empress Elizabeth's monogram

Imperial coat of arms – St. George and the double-headed eagle

Golden embroidery on red velvet

TSARS' SECRET POLICE

The notorious secret police of the tsars, the Third Department (later the Okhrana) infiltrated and suppressed revolutionary organizations. But the organization's cruelty pales beside the brutality of the Soviet secret police, the NKVD (later the KGB).

Carved and gilded female head

Like all Russian tsars, Alexander II was an accomplished horseman

ALEXANDER II

The highlight of Alexander's reign was the emancipation of the serfs in 1861. But the reforming tsar was killed by a terrorist's bomb in 1881. His successor, Alexander III, pursued harsh, reactionary policies, reversing many of his father's reforms.

Nicholas and Alexandra wear 17th-century tsarist costumes for a grand ball, 1903

STRONG EMPRESSES, WEAK EMPERORS

After the death of Peter I in 1725, the rest of the 18th century was dominated by strong empresses, among them Peter I's daughter, Elizabeth, and German-born Catherine II. Assisted by elite guards, each took the throne by force from weak emperors, and both enjoyed the popularity of the general public. The ornate decoration of Elizabeth's gilded throne (above) is typical of her extravagant taste. Both Elizabeth and Catherine were responsible for most of the opulent palaces and royal estates in and around St. Petersburg.

LAST IN LINE

Nicholas II celebrated the 300th anniversary of the Romanov dynasty in 1913. Four years later, however, he abdicated on behalf of himself and his hemophilic son following the catastrophe of war and civil rioting. The tsar and his family were murdered by the Bolsheviks in 1918 (p.32).

Empire building

THE HISTORY OF Russia is one of almost continual expansion. It has been estimated that from 1600 to 1900 Russia grew at a rate of 50 square miles (130 square km) a day! With no natural barriers to the east or west, Russia lay open to repeated invasions throughout its history. After gaining strength, Russia expanded its frontiers, partly to protect its vulnerable heartland. By the end of the 18th century, Russia included Siberia, western Ukraine, Lithuania, Poland, and Tatar Crimea. In 1809, Finland was added, and in the first half of the 19th century, the small countries of the Caucasus – Georgia, Armenia, and Azerbaijan – and huge areas of Central Asia became part of the empire.

FOUNDER OF THE RUSSIAN FLEET
Peter the Great, the first tsar to interest himself in naval matters, founded the Russian fleet after studying shipbuilding in Holland and England. In the Great Northern War with Sweden (1700–21) he expanded Russian territory to the Baltic Sea, gaining Swedish territory in southern Finland, the marshes on which he built his new capital, St. Petersburg, and what are now Estonia and Latvia. Peter the Great also captured the long peninsula of Kamchatka and the Kurile Islands in the Pacific Ocean.

Hatpin of Ukrainian Cossack leader Bogdan Khmelnitsky

Brass gun barrel

Porcelain cup showing General Bagration

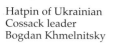

Type of cannon employed at the Battle of Borodino

BAGRATION AT BORODINO
Leading a French army half a million strong, Napoleon invaded Russia in June 1812. By September, he had succeeded in reaching Borodino on the approaches to Moscow. A bloody battle broke out in which many were mortally wounded, including one of the most brilliant commanders of the Russian army, a Georgian prince, Pyotr Bagration. Afterward, the Russians, led by the crafty, one-eyed Marshal Mikhail Kutuzov, retreated. Napoleon took Moscow but was driven out in October.

Wooden wheels are strengthened with metal

IMPERIAL EMPIRE

By 1914 the Russian empire was by far the largest in the world, stretching from the Arctic Ocean to the Caspian Sea and from the Baltic Sea to the Pacific. Within its borders were diverse nationalities ranging from the northern ice-bound Chukchi to the desert nomads of Kazakhstan. The huge empire, which included Finland and Poland, was divided into provinces and ruled from St. Petersburg.

Defense of Sevastopol 1854–55

CRIMEAN WAR

In the Crimean War (1853–56), Russia fought against Britain, France, and Turkey. Russia, badly led and poorly supplied, was defeated despite the heroic year-long defense of Sevastopol, on the Black Sea, and a naval victory against Turkey. Under the peace treaty, Russia kept the Crimea, but its power in the Black Sea was weakened.

EXPLORING ALASKA

Fur-rich Alaska, separated from Siberia by narrow straits, was first visited by Russians in 1741. In 1789 Joseph Billings, an English sailor in Russian service, led a secret expedition to study Alaska's peoples and explore its coast. The United States bought Alaska in 1867.

Letter of July 1791 carved on walrus tusk, and sent to Billings from Siberia, documents landings on Alaskan coast

RUNAWAY SERFS

The first Cossacks were runaway serfs and outlaws who formed frontier settlements in southern Russia and Ukraine. At first, Cossacks opposed the Russian authorities, but by the 19th century they had turned their settlements into prosperous agricultural communities and were fiercely loyal to the tsar.

Cossack *shashka* sword

CONQUEST OF SIBERIA

Ivan the Terrible opened the way to the resources of Siberia when he defeated the Tatars at Kazan on the Volga. Yermak, a daring Cossack leader, penetrated farther into fur-rich western Siberia in 1581, as shown in Surikov's painting of 1895. With 840 men he conquered the native tribes and greatly expanded Russia's borders.

Cannons were dragged to their battle positions by horses

MILITARY COSSACKS

Cossacks wore distinctive uniforms, with tall fur hats and sheepskin cloaks; they carried a sword (like this *shashka*, right) and a long lance. All Cossack men had to serve in Cossack military units, which were famous for their loyalty, bravery, and fine horsemanship.

DEFEAT OF NAPOLEON

In 1812, the French took Moscow. But a terrible fire destroyed most of the city, including winter supplies. After just a month Napoleon, the conqueror of Europe and Egypt, was forced to retreat. Frozen and starving, 90 percent of his men died or deserted. Two years later, the Russians, under Alexander I, rode triumphantly into Paris and Russia began to play a prominent role in European affairs.

Life at court

Scepter is decorated with the Orlov diamond, one of the largest in the world

IN MUSCOVITE TIMES (pp. 8–9) the royal court was at the Kremlin in Moscow. Tsars were attended by bearded *boyars* (nobles), wearing ornate costumes. Elaborate court rituals, such as the deep kowtow (bow), were based on Byzantine customs and those of the former Mongol overlords. The imperial court at St. Petersburg (1712–1917) adopted Western dress and manners, imitating French King Louis XIV's opulent court of Versailles. The Russian emperor or empress was attended by French-speaking aristocrats.

SILVER SPECTACLES
Catherine the Great was a prodigious reader, correspondent, and writer of plays. She used these elegant spectacles (with their enamel case) when working at her desk.

CROWN JEWELS
The diamond-studded Grand Imperial Crown of 1762, made for Catherine II's enthronement, was used in all subsequent coronations. The central band of diamond oak leaves and acorns, symbols of state power, begins with Empress Elizabeth's perfect diamond of 56 carats and ends with a magnificent Chinese ruby of nearly 400 carats.

Gilt cupids adorn the front of the carriage

CORONATION CEREMONY
The crowning of Nicholas II in 1896, shown above, took place at the Assumption Cathedral, Moscow. Coronations continued to be held in the cathedral after the capital moved to St. Petersburg. Nicholas II's coronation celebrations were horribly marred when 1,200 peasants were killed in a stampede of people waiting to receive royal gifts.

GRAND PALACE BALLS
From the elegant dances held by Alexander I to the sumptuous fancy-dress affairs of the fun-loving Elizabeth, lavish balls were the highlight of the winter season in St. Petersburg. Olga, Nicholas II's eldest daughter, made her debut in 1913 at the last glittering ball held before the Bolshevik Revolution.

Wooden wheels with metal rims

Two or three pairs of matched horses would have drawn the carriage

IVORY HUNTING GUN

Hunting was a favorite pastime of the court. The fine workmanship of Empress Catherine's gun, made in about 1780 at Tula, south of Moscow, is typical of the skill of Russian craftsmen. There is a famous legend that when English smiths gave Nicholas I a miniature dancing steel flea, the expert Tula craftsmen responded by fitting it with tiny boots.

Steel barrel

Flintlock mechanism

Gold-embossed ivory grip

Emperor Paul

FANCIFUL FABERGÉ

Peter Carl Fabergé, a St. Petersburg jeweler of French origin, made spectacular and intricate ornaments. Every year Nicholas II ordered Easter eggs for his wife and mother. This egg, with 18 miniature portraits of the tsars, was made in 1913 to celebrate the Romanov dynasty.

Peter the Great

Nicholas II

Elegant wooden canopy decorated with gilt laurel and oak leaves

Coachman sits on velvet-draped box while controlling the horses

Carved golden eagle acts as a guardian

System of leather straps supports the body of the carriage

Scenes of cupids and goddesses are painted on the side panels

CATHERINE'S CARRIAGE

Catherine the Great's lover, Count Grigory Orlov, organized the coup against her husband. He presented the empress with this ornate summer carriage, made of gilded wood and painted with scenes on the paneled back and sides. On ceremonial occasions elegant horse-drawn carriages would fill the streets leading to the Winter Palace or the Kremlin in seemingly endless processions.

Back wheels are larger than front wheels for easy turning

City of domes

Central octagonal tower is topped by a small gold cupola

AFTER THE TATARS' DEFEAT in 1380, Moscow gained in power and, by the 15th century, had become the leading city of Russia. Although Peter the Great moved the capital to St. Petersburg in 1712, Moscow, the "second capital," still played a major role. In 1812 Napoleon captured Moscow. But the city was soon ablaze – probably set on fire deliberately by its citizens, who preferred to flee rather than surrender. Napoleon's starving army, faced with the onset of winter, was then forced to retreat. The rebuilt city prospered, and became the capital again in 1918, under the Bolsheviks. Before the October Revolution, Moscow was known for its amazing domed churches, but half were destroyed during the Soviet era. In the new Russia, many are being rebuilt.

CITY FOUNDER
Moscow was founded by Prince Yury Dolgoruky. It is first mentioned in early Russian chronicles in 1147, when Dolgoruky invited other princes to a feast. The first wooden fortress was built in 1156, on the hill where the Kremlin now stands.

Kremlin   *W*   *Red Square*

S   *N*

E

CITY BOUNDARIES
This 1605 map shows how Moscow developed in a circular pattern. Expanding eastward from the Kremlin to embrace Red Square, the city then widened in a walled horseshoe around the original core. Wooden palisades (fences) and dirt ramparts (embankments) were built in 1592 to circle the whole wooden town. This old town center now makes up only 2 percent of the modern city.

ST. BASIL'S CATHEDRAL
Dominating Red Square is the fantastic Cathedral of the Intercession, better known as St. Basil's. It is named after a holy man who dared to stand up to Ivan the Terrible. The cathedral was built between 1555 and 1561 to celebrate Ivan's victory over the Tatars. It consists of eight chapels topped by ornate domes grouped around the central church tower. Ivan allegedly blinded the architects to ensure that this masterpiece could never be rivaled.

All Saints Gate guarding the bridge across the Moscow River

Ivan Veliky bell tower, for many years the tallest building in Moscow

Medieval palaces, including the tsars' Terem Palace

All Saints, or Great Stone, Bridge, built in 1692

VIEW OF THE KREMLIN
The Kremlin, the high-walled triangular fortress on the Moscow River, shines with 33 golden domes and contains the great cathedrals and former palaces of the tsars. Italian Renaissance architects built the walls and most of the churches between 1475 and 1505. After the 1917 Revolution, Lenin, and then Stalin, lived and worked in the Kremlin. Today it houses the office of the Russian president.

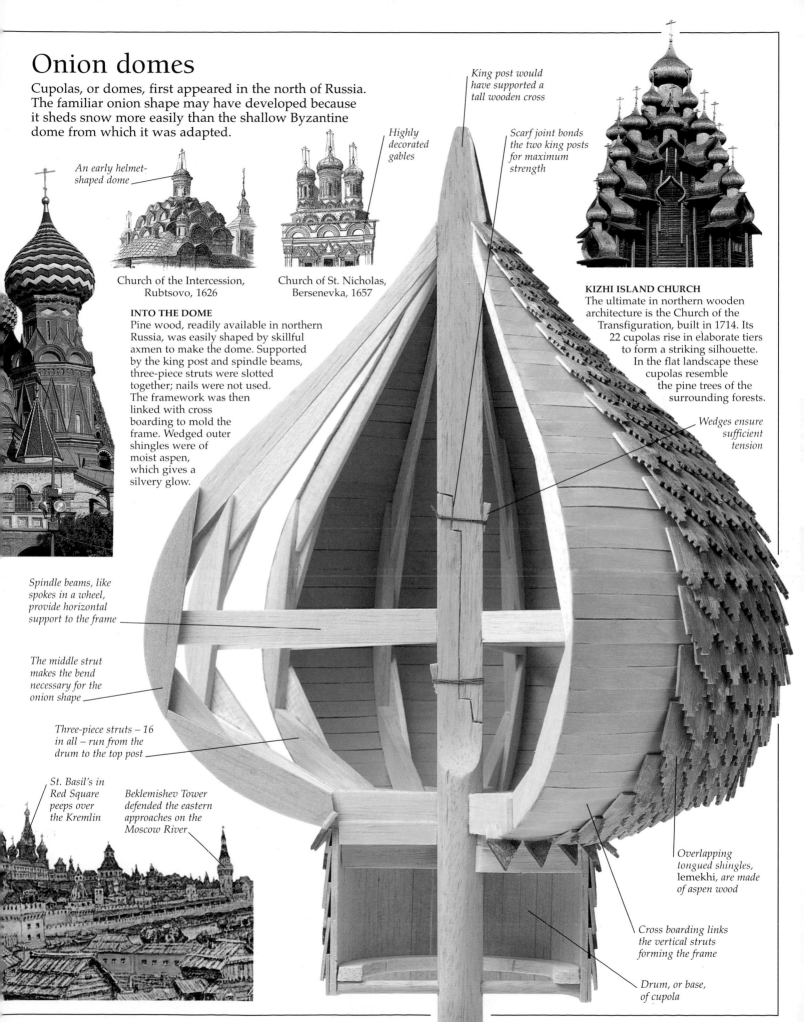

Onion domes

Cupolas, or domes, first appeared in the north of Russia. The familiar onion shape may have developed because it sheds snow more easily than the shallow Byzantine dome from which it was adapted.

An early helmet-shaped dome

Church of the Intercession, Rubtsovo, 1626

Highly decorated gables

Church of St. Nicholas, Bersenevka, 1657

INTO THE DOME
Pine wood, readily available in northern Russia, was easily shaped by skillful axmen to make the dome. Supported by the king post and spindle beams, three-piece struts were slotted together; nails were not used. The framework was then linked with cross boarding to mold the frame. Wedged outer shingles were of moist aspen, which gives a silvery glow.

King post would have supported a tall wooden cross

Scarf joint bonds the two king posts for maximum strength

KIZHI ISLAND CHURCH
The ultimate in northern wooden architecture is the Church of the Transfiguration, built in 1714. Its 22 cupolas rise in elaborate tiers to form a striking silhouette. In the flat landscape these cupolas resemble the pine trees of the surrounding forests.

Wedges ensure sufficient tension

Spindle beams, like spokes in a wheel, provide horizontal support to the frame

The middle strut makes the bend necessary for the onion shape

Three-piece struts – 16 in all – run from the drum to the top post

St. Basil's in Red Square peeps over the Kremlin

Beklemishev Tower defended the eastern approaches on the Moscow River

Overlapping tongued shingles, lemekhi, are made of aspen wood

Cross boarding links the vertical struts forming the frame

Drum, or base, of cupola

Palaces of St. Petersburg

Crossed anchors are St. Petersburg's coat of arms

Gilded spire

Building began in 1712 but was not completed until 1733

Receding tiers with volutes (scrolls) like Dutch buildings

ON THE MARSHY banks of the River Neva, Peter the Great built his new capital, St. Petersburg. He wanted to give Russia an outlet to the sea and a "window to the west." By 1712 he had succeeded, but thousands had died of fevers and exhaustion in the process. St. Petersburg is a place of palaces and spires, reflecting the European classical style of its many foreign architects. During World War II over a million citizens died as a result of a nearly three-year blockade by the German army. St. Petersburg became Petrograd between 1914 and 1924, then Leningrad until 1991, when the original name was restored.

Alexander Column is a memorial to the 1812 victory over Napoleon

THE ARCHITECT RASTRELLI
The Italian Bartolomeo Rastrelli (1700–71) was court architect under Empresses Anna and Elizabeth. He built stunning royal palaces of astonishing size and color, with lavish interiors. But his work fell out of favor with Catherine II, who preferred classical architecture.

FROZEN FONTANKA
Lined by grand houses, the Fontanka River is one of four rivers and canals that emerge from the Neva to loop through the center of the old city. In winter the Fontanka freezes so hard that it is able to support vehicles.

CITY LAYOUT
St. Petersburg is grouped around narrow rivers and canals with the broad Neva River at the center. Large islands like the Vasilievsky on the left and Hare Island, where the fortress stands, face the mainland. Nevsky Prospekt is the most important of the streets that radiate from the Neva River.

PETER AND PAUL FORTRESS
The fortress, begun in 1703, was the first building constructed in the city. Rising from its center is the Cathedral of Saints Peter and Paul. With its tall, slim spire, it symbolizes the city as much as St. Basil's does Moscow.

Top floor of the palace was used as servants' quarters

WINTER PALACE
The magnificent Winter Palace, begun in 1754 for Empress Elizabeth and completed in 1762, is Rastrelli's crowning achievement. It is a closed square with a spacious courtyard built on the banks of the Neva River. It burned down in 1837 but within a year was rebuilt almost exactly as before. Long the main residence of the tsars, the Winter Palace became the Hermitage Museum after the Revolution.

GRAND INTERIORS
Rich interiors like this palatial dining room are often found in 18th- and 19th-century palaces, not only of the tsars but also of high-ranking members of the aristocracy. Marble columns are used in abundance in halls based on Greek and Roman architecture. Precious materials such as amber decorate the walls, and gold leaf is found everywhere.

Ornate cupolas can be seen from a considerable distance

Elaborate window frames are typical of Rastrelli

CATHERINE PALACE
These gold cupolas belong to the chapel of the Catherine Palace. This royal summer residence stands at Tsarskoe Selo, on the outskirts of St. Petersburg. It was designed by Rastrelli for Empress Elizabeth and named after her mother. The palace's landscaped gardens were laid out during the reign of Catherine the Great.

SMOLNY CONVENT
Rastrelli was responsible for Empress Elizabeth's Convent of the Resurrection. Its first ornate buildings were completed in 1764, after Elizabeth's death. In contrast to the extravagant exterior, the interior was left undecorated. Catherine II confiscated the convent to use it for Russia's first girls' school, whose students were young noblewomen. The school later became the headquarters of Lenin's Bolsheviks; here he planned the October 1917 Revolution.

Gilt Peterhof statue

PETERHOF
Peterhof, on the Gulf of Finland, was Peter the Great's favorite summer residence. The palace, modeled on the French palace and gardens at Versailles, was begun in 1714 and was later added to by Rastrelli. The Grand Cascade of fountains was adorned with many gilded statues. The palace and grounds were ruined during World War II but have been beautifully restored.

Grand Cascade of fountains

Gold cupola pinpoints position of the palace cathedral

Catherine II's rooms were on the second floor, in the southeast corner

Bolshevik Revolution

AFTER RIOTS in Petrograd (St. Petersburg until 1914) in February 1917, Nicholas II abdicated the throne and a Provisional Government took over. The Revolution had many causes. In 1905, widespread discontent erupted in strikes, uprisings, and mutinies. Food shortages, the tsar's weak leadership, and Russia's disastrous performance in World War I heightened unrest. Failure to stop the war angered soldiers and peasants, and in October 1917 the Bolshevik (Communist) Party, led by Vladimir Lenin, seized power. Lenin dissolved the Provisional Government and made peace with Germany at the cost of huge territories, including Ukraine.

GRIGORI RASPUTIN
The fake holy man Grigori Rasputin gained huge influence over Nicholas II and Empress Alexandra because of his apparent ability to cure the hemophilia attacks of their son and heir, Alexei. While the tsar was at the front during World War I, Rasputin virtually ruled Russia. In 1916 the unpopular Rasputin was murdered by relatives of the tsar.

Peaceful demonstrators slain by tsar's troops

WORKERS UNITE
In Moscow, the 1917 Revolution was very violent compared to the almost bloodless coup in Petrograd. Militant workers fought fiercely against the stronger forces of cadets loyal to the Provisional Government. Only after ten days of furious fighting around the Kremlin did the Bolsheviks emerge triumphant in Russia's second capital.

Blank shots fired from the Aurora *signaled the start of the Bolshevik uprising*

"BLOODY SUNDAY"
On January 9, 1905, a young priest, Father Gapon, led workers from St. Petersburg's factories to the Winter Palace to petition the tsar. Hundreds of peaceful demonstrators, including women and children, were killed when soldiers opened fire. The massacre shook the nation's faith in the tsar.

WWI Russian troops wear gas masks while fighting in the trenches

WORLD WAR I
Russia, an ally of France and Britain, entered World War I in 1914. Russia's troops fought bravely and at first won important victories against Austria and Germany. But her armies lacked adequate supplies and later suffered defeats, with heavy casualties and desertions. Popular enthusiasm gave way to disillusion and war-weariness.

SIGNAL FOR THE REVOLUTION
The sailors of the cruiser *Aurora* mutinied against their officers in March 1917 and joined the Bolsheviks. Anchored on the River Neva in central Petrograd, the *Aurora* fired a blank shot on October 25, 1917. The shot signaled the storming of the almost undefended Winter Palace, where the remaining members of the Provisional Government were meeting.

LEON TROTSKY

The dynamic revolutionary Leon Trotsky was imprisoned and then banished for his part in the 1905 Revolution. He escaped abroad and joined the Bolsheviks in 1917. Trotsky was the main organizer, with Lenin, of the October Revolution. He became commissar (head) of foreign affairs, and then of war, and went on to organize and lead the Red Army during the Civil War.

Official stamp making document legal

Membership number

Issued to Comrade Andrei Andreev

Joined the Party on September 2, 1912

Member was most likely exempt from monthly payments since none are logged

COMMUNIST PARTY MEMBERSHIP

Lenin's party was known as the Social Democratic Labor Party until 1919, when it was renamed the Communist Party. Its members were called Bolsheviks. This membership ticket belonged to Andrei Andreev, who joined the Party in 1912. He was a member of its top policy-making committee, the Politburo, from 1932 to 1952. He was one of the few Old Bolsheviks to survive Stalin's purges (pp. 35, 36).

BOLSHEVIK LEADER

Vladimir Lenin, a revolutionary since student days, was banished to Siberia in 1897. He believed that workers had to rebel against the establishment to create a fair society. In 1900 Lenin went abroad, where he began a ruthless campaign to gain total control of the exiled Russian Social Democratic Labor Party. The party split: Lenin's group, the "Bolsheviks" (majority), opposed the "Mensheviks" (minority).

In 1917 Lenin returned to Russia to lead the Bolshevik Revolution.

TOPPLING OF THE TSARS

Many tsarist symbols were destroyed after the Bolshevik Revolution. Nicholas II's huge statue of his father, Alexander III, was toppled in 1918. Lenin, who ordered it to be destroyed, never forgot that his elder brother had been executed for plotting to assassinate Tsar Alexander.

Medal marks the 15th anniversary of the Revolution

PETROGRAD GUARDS

The Red Guards were armed units, mostly of factory workers, who played a key part in seizing power for the Bolsheviks. This medal was awarded to Red Guards who defended Petrograd during the Revolution and Civil War (pp. 32–33).

The Civil War

Imperial helmet plate

THE COMPARATIVELY bloodless October Revolution (pp. 30–31) was followed by a cruel civil war between the anti-Communist White Army and the Bolshevik Red Army. The White forces lacked strong leadership but, aided by Western powers, enjoyed early successes. In 1920, however, the Red Army, joined by many tsarist officers, was victorious. Although the Bolsheviks lost Poland, Finland, and the Baltic states, the rest of the Russian empire remained within the new Communist state. The horror of civil war was followed by a terrible famine, relieved only by U.S. aid. In 1921, to restore the ruined country, Lenin announced the New Economic Policy. This reintroduced private trade.

WAR BOATS
River steamers like this one, rechristened *Vanya the Communist*, were taken over for use in the Civil War. The boat was destroyed in a fierce battle on the River Kama in October 1918.

Shield protects machine-gun operator from enemy bullets

Imperial sword

Execution of Tsar Nicholas II

"Workers of all countries unite! In struggle you will win justice!"

Machine gun mounted on a former private carriage

SLAUGHTER OF THE ROMANOVS
In July 1918, the White forces threatened Yekaterinburg in Siberia, where the Bolsheviks were holding Nicholas II, the former tsar. Early on July 17, 1918, by Lenin's order, the tsar and his family were murdered. Their bodies, burned and buried in a pit in the forest, were not discovered until 1992.

WORDS OF MARX
This Bolshevik banner quotes the words of Karl Marx, who, in his *Communist Manifesto* (statement of aims), urged the workers to unite since they had nothing to lose but their chains. After the October Revolution, however, power went not to the workers but to the Communist Party leaders.

Tsarist Imperial Army badge

WHITES AGAINST REDS
White Army soldiers were against the Communist takeover for a variety of reasons: some still supported the tsarist regime; some wanted the Provisional Government (p. 30) to be restored; while others were completely opposed to Bolshevik ideas.

RED ARMY TROOPS
The ill-disciplined voluntary Red Guards were transformed into the Red Army by the brilliant commander Leon Trotsky. He appointed former tsarist officers and reintroduced order and distinctions between officers and soldiers. He kept close contact with the army by traveling quickly to areas of conflict in his armored train.

Flaps can be turned down to keep ears warm in winter

ARMY RECRUITMENT
Mass conscription (the draft) meant that many army recruits came straight from the countryside with little or no military training. They were reluctant soldiers: many deserted the army and returned to their villages, especially at harvest time.

"I am a plowman on guard, with my rifle I stand, I preserve freedom and my land"

Red Army cap badge, 1919

Sight aligns eye with target

DRESSED TO KILL
Red Army uniforms were haphazard affairs. Many soldiers wore their own clothes, or captured White uniforms, and crude birch-bark *lapti* shoes instead of boots. The pointed hat with the star, called a *budyonovka* after Marshal Budyonny, came to symbolize the Red Army soldier.

Order of the Red Banner, 1921

MARSHAL BUDYONNY
This pistol belonged to Red Army commander Marshal Budyonny, a former officer in the Imperial Cavalry. His skilled horsemanship in battle became legendary.

Seat for soldiers

RED COMMISSAR
Commissars were Party members attached to Red Army units to ensure political loyalty. They carried arms and were better dressed than most army members.

Document case for paperwork

Carriage was drawn by horses

Metal-rimmed wooden wheels made it difficult to maneuver the carriage on rough terrain

CIVIL WAR CARRIAGE
The *tachanka*, a horse-drawn carriage with mounted machine gun, is typical of the makeshift methods of the chaotic Civil War. This *tachanka* was employed in a famous battle in which Germans, Poles, and Ukrainian nationalists fought for control of the Ukraine before the Reds finally won in 1920.

The rise of Stalin

WHEN LENIN DIED IN 1924, the struggle was on to inherit the leadership of the Communist Party. Trotsky, the most able candidate, was soon outmaneuvered by Joseph Stalin, the devious secretary general of the Party. Stalin joined with two other leaders to defeat Trotsky, then formed a new alliance to oust them as well. Trotsky was exiled in 1929. Stalin then strengthened his power by launching rapid industrialization and agricultural collectivization. The Great Terror began in earnest with the murder in 1934 of the leading Bolshevik, Sergei Kirov. The secret police, the NKVD (later the KGB), became all-powerful, directing mass arrests from their infamous headquarters in Moscow. All the famous Old Bolshevik leaders were tried or shot.

DESTRUCTION OF CHURCHES
Churches were not only closed but, by the late 1920s, began to be destroyed in large numbers. The massive Cathedral of Christ the Savior (p. 58) in Moscow was completed in 1883 as a memorial to the Russian victory over Napoleon. It was blown up in a huge explosion in 1931 to make way for the Palace of the Soviets (see below).

This 1920s cartoon reflects Lenin's wish to convert the world to Communism

LENIN'S FUNERAL TRAIN
When Lenin died in January 1924, his body was brought to Moscow by train for a huge public funeral. His body was embalmed (preserved) and placed in a specially built mausoleum (tomb) in Red Square, where you can still see it today. The mausoleum also served as a platform for Soviet leaders viewing the annual parades on May Day and November 7 (pp. 56–57).

Train was made at the Putilov factory in St. Petersburg, 1910

Renovated in 1923, the train became a memorial to Lenin in 1937

LENIN AND WORLD REVOLUTION
This cartoon of Lenin sweeping the world clean of priests, capitalists, and kings illustrates the Communist hope that the Revolution would spread around the world. But Communism was not successful abroad. At home Lenin persecuted merchants, monarchists, and priests, closed churches, and nationalized trade and industry.

Р.У. Ж.Д. У. 127

MONUMENTAL PALACE
This design for the Palace of the Soviets was drawn in the 1930s. It was to be the tallest building in the world. But only the foundations were laid since building problems and World War II halted construction.

Motherhood award could be attached to a chain and worn proudly as a necklace

MOTHERHOOD AWARDS

After the Bolshevik Revolution, the government supported women's freedom, but by the 1930s traditional roles of women as wives and mothers were emphasized. To encourage a higher birthrate, the Motherhood Medal was granted to women with five children; those producing ten were declared Heroine Mothers.

RULE OF STALIN

Joseph Stalin became leader after Lenin's death by outmaneuvering Trotsky, Lenin's natural successor, and other leaders. In the late 1920s he introduced forced collectivization of agriculture and rapid industrialization, which brought many hardships. Freedom of thought in the arts was also suppressed. Any remaining opposition was eliminated in the mass purges of 1937 (p. 36).

Hammer and sickle were adopted as emblems of the new state

COLLECTIVE FARMING

Collective farms combined small holdings into single units, often including several villages. Despite the invitation on this poster, peasants had no choice. In 1929 Stalin launched forced collectivization. The peasants resisted and millions died, or were shot or sent to labor camps. Production fell, causing a terrible famine. By 1938 collectivization had spread throughout the Soviet Union.

Stalin's real name was Dzhugashvili. Stalin comes from "stal," the Russian for steel; he adopted the name while he was working secretly for the early Bolsheviks

"Come to us in the collective farm!"

Soviet children were cared for in state crèches while their mothers worked

WOMEN'S ROLE

The new Soviet state granted women full legal equality. But by the 1930s the state became more authoritarian and women were expected to perform a dual role. They not only had to cook, clean, and shop for the family, but also do heavy manual labor on the farms or in the new factories. Childcare was organized to release women for work outside the home, but poor housing and lack of amenities made their lives arduous.

Stalin's mustache, simple clothes, and high leather boots were copied by the other leaders

Soviet Russia

DURING STALIN'S PURGES millions of innocent people were executed or sent to remote labor camps (*gulags*). These horrors were followed by the hardships of World War II. When the Soviet Union was invaded, Moscow nearly fell to the Germans and Leningrad suffered a long siege. After the war, good relations with Western allies deteriorated and the Cold War began. After Stalin's death in 1953, relations began to improve. But in 1962, Khrushchev built missile launch sites in Cuba, which led to a showdown with the U.S. Finally, after Gorbachev became Party leader in 1985 and introduced the policies of *glasnost* (freer speech) and *perestroika* (reform), the U.S.S.R. and the West grew friendly.

GERMAN INVASION
Breaking the Nazi-Soviet peace pact, Germany invaded the Soviet Union in June 1941. Stalin and the Red Army were taken by surprise and much of the western Soviet Union was occupied. But the Germans were turned back from Moscow, defeated at Stalingrad on the Volga in 1943, and pushed back to Berlin. They finally surrendered at Reims, France, on May 7, 1945. Two days later, Red Army soldiers gathered in front of the mausoleum in Red Square, Moscow, and threw captured Nazi flags before Stalin and other leaders.

Dzherzhinsky, founder of the Cheka, *the Soviet secret police*

STATE UNIVERSITY
The old Moscow University was expanded in Soviet times, and a large new university building was erected in the Lenin Hills. The building is one of Stalin's seven ornate, tiered skyscrapers, which changed the face of Moscow in the early 1950s. They are popularly known as wedding-cake palaces.

Constructed 1949–53, the central tower is 36 stories high

Mass grave marking from a gulag *near Karaganda in Central Asia*

The vast building contains not only departments and lecture halls but living quarters for the staff and students

LABOR CAMPS
Wooden grave tablets recorded only the burial sites – no prisoner names or numbers – of those who died in Stalin's labor camps (*gulags*). An estimated 20 million people were swallowed up in the huge concentration camp system.

Building's lower wings extend out from the center in U shapes

FOUNDER OF THE SECRET POLICE
Felix Dzerzhinsky was the first head of the Soviet secret police, then called the *Cheka*, after the 1917 Revolution. His hated statue (above), which stood on Lubyanka Square opposite the KGB headquarters in Moscow, was pulled down after the failed coup of 1991 (pp. 58–59). It now stands in a sculpture park in Moscow, along with statues of other leaders of the rejected Soviet regime.

CUBAN MISSILE CRISIS

In 1962, during the long Cold War (period of hostility between western countries and the Soviet Union), Soviet leader Nikita Khrushchev placed missiles in Cuba, within range of U.S. cities. Cuba, a Communist state ruled by Fidel Castro, was a strong supporter of the Soviet Union. U.S. President John F. Kennedy immediately ordered a naval blockade of Cuba. Six days later Khrushchev backed down; the missiles were removed. War had barely been avoided. The Communist Party's Central Committee forced Khrushchev to retire in 1964.

CONTROLLING THE ARTS

Under Stalin, writing, art, and even music had to praise Communism, Soviet life, and Stalin himself. *Worker and Peasant*, a sculpture by Vera Mukhina, was made for an exhibition in Paris in 1937.

Sickle symbolizes the agricultural worker

Hammer signifies the factory worker

Worker and Peasant, "looking into the glorious Communist future," was the symbol of Mosfilm, the large U.S.S.R. film studio

SOVIET SYMBOLS

Favorite themes for Soviet emblems were sheaves of wheat and the hammer and sickle used to decorate railings on one of Moscow's bridges. Portraits of the Party leader, hung on the walls of every office and institution, were changed when that leader fell out of favor. Instead of advertising, huge Party slogans decorated city streets and buildings.

The figures, made of stainless-steel panels, are young, strong, and attractive

Anniversary meeting of the Bolshevik Revolution took place here in 1941, as bombs fell outside during World War II

MOSCOW METRO

The construction of the Moscow subway was one of the engineering feats of the Stalin era. Its ornate stations were referred to as "palaces for the people." The first line opened in 1935 and each marble-lined station was decorated with sculptures or mosaics displaying a different theme. Most large cities in Russia now have a metro system. One of the most beautiful stations is Mayakovskaya (above).

Rail and industry

ALTHOUGH A LATE starter, by 1914 Russia had become the fifth largest industrial power in the world. After the Revolution and Civil War, production of manufactured goods fell sharply but rose again when Stalin launched his Five-Year Plans. However, tight government control left little room for new ideas, and Soviet Russia fell behind other modern economies. Industry was in crisis when the Soviet Union broke up in 1991, and production fell further when the new government moved abruptly to a market economy. In such a large country, the railroad network is vital. The first line, from Tsarskoe Selo to St. Petersburg, opened in 1837. By 1899 it had been extended east, greatly helping to open up the vast mineral wealth of Siberia.

"...TO WORK, COMRADES!"
Propaganda posters called on people to throw themselves into the work of the new factories. In 1929 Stalin's first Five-Year Plan was approved, under which rapid expansion of heavy industry was to be achieved by setting monthly and annual targets. In spite of tremendous hardships, by 1937 the Soviet Union had become the second largest industrial nation in the world.

Powerful lights enabled farmers to work through the night

Only the first tractors were fitted with wheel studs; later ones used caterpillar treads

COLLECTIVE FARMING
Industry was utilized to manufacture mineral fertilizers and farm machinery to meet the needs of the new collective and state farms. Traditional wooden farming implements (pp.16–17) were cast aside in favor of modern machinery.

Early Soviet tractors ran on diesel and were deliberately large for the enormous fields

FIRST SOVIET TRACTOR
This is the first tractor to roll off the production line of the Soviet Union's first tractor factory, which opened in 1930. Farm machinery was not kept on farms but at district "machine and tractor stations" (MTS's), which decided when and where they would be used. Until they were scrapped in 1957, MTS's kept the farms under tight political control.

Built in 1956, this was the last Soviet steam train

PASSENGER TRAINS

Russian trains are all electrified or use diesel engines. They have a wider gauge (track width) than European trains; the carriages – especially the sleeping cars – are more spacious, but cause problems at border crossings where the undercarriages have to be changed. There are no rapid trains as in Europe. The 404-mile (650-km) journey from Moscow to St. Petersburg takes five hours by express train.

LAYING THE TRACKS

Russia's first railroads were laid by thousands of workers using little more than pickaxes. During World War I, German prisoners of war built the important line to the ice-free port of Murmansk, above the Arctic Circle. The new line in eastern Siberia, the Baikal-Amur Magistral (BAM), completed in the 1980s, was built largely by volunteers from the *Komsomol* (Communist youth group).

RAILS ON PERMAFROST

It is very difficult to lay railroad lines in northern and eastern Russia, where the layer of permafrost (p. 11) can be almost 3,300 feet (1 km) thick and the earth is unstable during the short summer thaw. Nevertheless, rails have been successfully built beyond the Arctic Circle. They range as far as the coal-mining settlement at Vorkuta and the copper and nickel mines at Norilsk, where Stalin's concentration camps supplied forced labor from the 1930s to the 1950s.

TRANS-SIBERIAN RAILWAY

At 5,777 miles (9,297 km) the Trans-Siberian is the longest railroad line in the world. It runs from Moscow through Siberia to the Pacific, with spur lines to Mongolia and China. Building began in 1891 and was finally completed in 1916. Workers had to overcome terrible problems of terrain and climate as they laid tracks through forest and around the southern edge of huge Lake Baikal. The journey, which lasts 11 days, brings home to travelers the enormous expanse of Russia.

УЛААНБААТАР — МОСКВА

The Soviet T-34 was regarded as the best tank of World War II

Tank is painted white for camouflage in the snow

MASS-PRODUCED WEAPONS

At the start of World War II, hundreds of factories were moved east to the Urals and Siberia, beyond the reach of the invading German army. Tractor factories were adapted to produce tanks, including the T-34, which played a big part in Russia's victory. After the war, Soviet industry continued to mass-produce weapons – over 20 percent of the country's budget was spent on defense. In the new Russia, military spending has declined.

Kapitza's lenses

Science pioneers

RUSSIA HAS A LONG record of outstanding scientific achievement. In the 19th century Russian scientists made important advances in chemistry, radiotelegraphy, and mathematics. In the Soviet era, military science and space technology had priority, but political interference and unjustified arrests of scientists stifled progress. In 1980 Andrei Sakharov, whose theories enabled the Soviets to build a hydrogen bomb, was exiled for defending human rights. Russia was first to send an artificial satellite, and then a person, into space.

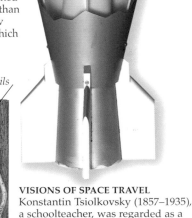

Living quarters on this model spaceship are above – control rooms below

Distillation jar used in experiments by Lomonosov

FATHER OF AVIATION
Nikolai Zhukovsky (1847–1921) is often called the father of Russian aviation. In the early days of flying he pioneered the study of aerodynamics. In 1905, he figured out how to calculate the lifting power of an airplane; later, he developed the whirlwind theory, on which helicopter flight is based.

ATOMIC THEORIST
Mikhail Lomonosov (1711–65) was the greatest scientist of his day. A pioneering chemist and physicist, he anticipated part of the atomic theory two centuries before it was fully described. He was also a poet and a founder of Moscow University.

PAVLOV'S SALIVATING DOGS
As a physiologist, Ivan Pavlov (1849–1936) studied the brain, the nervous system, and digestion. By repeatedly sounding a bell at meal times, he trained a dog to salivate at the sound of the bell, rather than at the arrival of food. Through this study, Pavlov developed the theory of conditioned reflexes, which he later applied to humans. He won a Nobel Prize in 1904.

Metal filings in the coherer detect electrical waves and send signals via wires to coils

FIRST RUSSIAN RADIO
Alexander Popov (1859–1905), a physicist, invented the antenna (aerial). In 1895 he made his first radio, right, on which a message could be sent via an antenna to a receiver. The protoype still works. The invention greatly improved communications between ship and shore and assisted in the development of the telephone. Also, telegrams could now be sent by radio waves instead of over cables. The Italian physicist Guglielmo Marconi, who knew of Popov's experiments, patented a radio at about the same time.

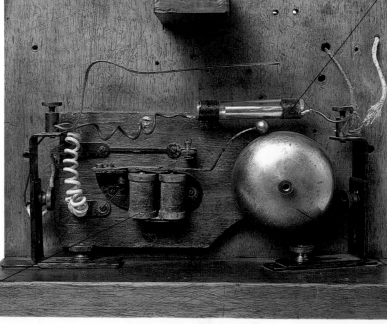

Electrical coils connect to a large battery at the back

VISIONS OF SPACE TRAVEL
Konstantin Tsiolkovsky (1857–1935), a schoolteacher, was regarded as a dreamer for imagining space travel nearly a century before it happened. In 1903 Tsiolkovsky designed this spaceship and correctly wrote the theory of rocket power. In the 1920s, Tsiolkovsky developed the idea of jet engines, and proposed that rockets propelled by liquid fuel could be used to send ships into space. But the technology that would make space travel a reality was not available during his lifetime.

Bell sounds when tapped by the stimulated electrical coils

KAPITZA'S PHYSICS
Pyotr Kapitza (1894–1984) won a Nobel Prize in 1978 for his work on low-temperature physics. Kapitza worked in England in the 1920s and 1930s. On a visit home in 1934, Stalin made him stay in the Soviet Union. From 1946 until Stalin's death, Kapitza was under house arrest for refusing to work on the atomic bomb. But he kept up his research using handmade apparatus.

Cartoon of Kapitza, 1971

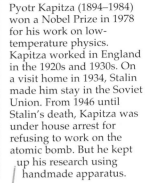

This tiny thermos could hold liquid helium at the low temperatures needed for Kapitza's research

Balloon basket in which Mendeleyev watched an eclipse of the sun

Four extendable aerials protrude from aluminum sphere

SOVIET SATELLITE
On October 4, 1957, to the astonishment of the world, the Soviet Union launched Sputnik I. Designed by the brilliant rocket and engine scientists Sergei Korolev and Valentin Glushko, Sputnik was the first artificial satellite; it made one full orbit of the earth. The Space Age had begun; ultimately people landed on the moon, and unmanned probes reached Mars, Venus, and Jupiter.

Aluminum sphere contains a radio transmitter

MENDELEYEV'S BALLOON
Dmitry Mendeleyev (1834–1907) was an unusual combination of a great scientist and a successful businessman. He drew up the periodic table of chemical elements, fundamental to the study of chemistry. He also did pioneering work in crystallography and on petroleum, gases, and liquids. Among his main interests were meteorology and astronomy. When an eclipse of the sun occurred over Russia in 1887, Mendeleyev went up alone in this balloon basket to closely observe and take notes on the phenomenon.

FIRST IN SPACE
Only four years after the launch of Sputnik I, the Russian Yuri Gagarin (1934–68) became the first person in space. On April 12, 1961, he was launched into orbit aboard the capsule Vostok I, and made one circuit of the globe in 1 hour and 48 minutes before ejecting from the capsule and returning to earth by parachute. Gagarin died a few years later, when his jet plane crashed during a training flight.

Media and communications

CONTEMPORARY RUSSIAN USES the Cyrillic alphabet, which was developed in the 9th century to provide a written language for Slavic people. Largely based on the Greek script, Cyrillic also shares many letters with the Latin alphabet. The first Russian book was printed in 1563. Shortly afterward, moralizing tales in comic-strip form (*lubok*) were printed. These were the earliest form of popular newspapers; they remained popular until the 19th century. At the beginning of the 20th century, as more people learned to read, regular newspapers became common and book publication greatly expanded. Soviet Russia made great efforts to develop radio, cinema, and television – partly because of their value in spreading state propaganda.

POSTAL SYSTEM
Russia had a primitive postal system as early as the 13th century. By the 17th century the mail was better organized, with post stations providing fresh horses at stages along major routes. In 1874 Russia joined the International Postal Union. The modern system serves the whole vast country using air, rail, and water transport.

Although buried for centuries, the writing is still legible

Birch bark is flattened for ease of writing

BIRCH-BARK TABLET
By the 13th century the northern city-state of Novgorod enjoyed a high standard of literacy, and even a form of democracy. Paper was not yet in common use, so messages were sent on pieces of birch bark, such as this one which conveys greetings to a citizen of Novgorod. These ancient letters were dug up by archaeologists from the University of Moscow in 1960.

Amplifier for broadcasting sound

Large wooden box containing receiver circuits

АБВГДЕ
ЁЖЗИЙ
КЛМНО
ПРСТУФ
ХЦЧШЩ
ЪЫЬЭЮЯ

CYRILLIC SCRIPT
The Russian alphabet is known as Cyrillic after St. Cyril. He and his brother, St. Methodius, adapted the Greek alphabet in the 9th century to provide a written language for Slavic people. Cyrillic's 33 letters match all the vowels and consonants used in Russian speech. This means the language is written just as it is spoken and is very easy to spell and pronounce correctly.

НЕГРАМОТНЫЙ ТОТ-ЖЕ СЛЕПОЙ
ВСЮДУ ЕГО ЖДУТ НЕУДАЧИ И НЕСЧАСТЬЯ.

PROMOTING LITERACY
Before the reforms of Alexander II (p. 17), most Russians could not read or write. The opening of new schools meant that by 1917 over 40 percent of the nation was literate. This poster was part of the Bolshevik campaign of the 1920s to achieve 100 percent literacy.

GOING TO PRINT
Ivan Fyodorov, who printed the first Russian book in 1563, was run out of Moscow by the scribes, who were afraid of losing their jobs. In the early years of the 20th century, as people became more literate, a great expansion took place in book and newspaper printing.

SPREADING THE WORD
The phototelegraph, a technological advance in 1975, meant newspaper proofs could be sent quickly to every major city for simultaneous printing. It aided the centralized Soviet system as Party and government newspapers could appear at the same time in every city of the Soviet Union.

Knob for adjusting the picture

Viewing screen is just 1.18 in (3 cm) wide

On/off button

Volume control

COMMUNIST NEWS
The increase in literacy at the beginning of the 20th century led to the widespread availability of newspapers. *Pravda* began publication in a very small way in 1912 but reached a circulation of over 5 million during the Soviet era. Although its name means "truth," *Pravda* reported only what the Communist Party wanted the people to know, and facts were often ignored or distorted. The main mouthpiece of the Communist Party, the newspaper has survived in the new Russia but with a much reduced circulation.

EARLY TELEVISION
In 1931 the first Soviet television set was produced; it had only a tiny round screen. Transmissions began that year and by 1938 regular programs were being broadcast in Moscow and Leningrad. But only in the 1960s did television become available throughout the country. Like other areas of Soviet life, television was highly controlled and focused on the capital, with the same programs being relayed nationwide.

DOCUMENTING HISTORY
Sergei Eisenstein's films of the 1920s and 1930s are among the world's greatest. The scene above is from *October* (1927), about the Bolshevik Revolution. Under Stalin, filmmaking was rigidly controlled, but after his death exceptional films appeared again. These included Andrei Tarkovsky's *Rublev* (1966), about a famous icon painter, and Tengiz Abuladze's *Repentance* (1987), which deals with Stalinist terror.

Famous writers

RUSSIA'S FIRST-RECORDED literature was the 12th-century heroic poem, *The Song of Igor's Campaign*, about the capture of a Russian prince. But it was in the 19th century that Russian writing became world-famous. Pushkin and Mikhail Lermontov wrote fine romantic poetry and stories. Gogol's biting stories and the great novels of Tolstoy and Dostoevsky continued the Pushkin tradition. The last of the great 19th-century masters was Chekhov, who wrote brilliant plays and short stories. This great literary tradition continued in the 20th century with novels by Mikhail Bulgakov, Pasternak, and Solzhenitsyn, and the poetry of Anna Akhmatova and Osip Mandelstam, as well as new works by women writers, such as Lyudmila Petrushevskaya and Tatiana Tolstaya.

Quill pen with which Gogol wrote Dead Souls

Script of Gogol's story "A Terrible Vengeance," about a woman who falls under the spell of her father, a wizard

NIKOLAI GOGOL
Gogol (1809–52) was a dramatist, novelist, and short story writer. His works were a mixture of fantasy, horror, and humor. Gogol wrote about Cossacks and of life in the Ukraine. But his greatest works were *The Inspector General*, a play that made fun of provincial officials, and *Dead Souls*, a witty novel about serfs and landowners. Gogol burned his second volume of *Dead Souls* after a fanatical priest convinced him that the work was evil. Gogol died several days later – perhaps depriving the world of another masterpiece.

ALEXANDER PUSHKIN
Pushkin (1799–1837) is considered Russia's greatest poet. He was banished in 1824 for revolutionary and anti-religious writings. While barred from the capital, Pushkin was looked after by his nanny, about whom he wrote the poem "Companion in My Austere Days." Among his greatest works are the historical play *Boris Godunov*; a long poem, *The Bronze Horseman*, about a tragic flood in St. Petersburg; and many wonderful lyrical poems, which most Russians know by heart. Pushkin died, aged 37, fighting a duel, like the one in his greatest work, *Eugene Onegin*, against one of his beautiful wife's admirers.

Silver tea strainer given to Pushkin by his nanny

FYODOR DOSTOEVSKY
Dostoevsky (1821–81) is one of the world's greatest novelists but was often very poor. He was arrested in 1849 for belonging to a secret intellectual group, and sentenced to death. While standing before the firing squad, Dostoevsky was pardoned and sent to Siberia. His terrible experiences are reflected in his account of prison life, *The House of the Dead*. He also wrote *Crime and Punishment*, a novel about a murder.

ANTON CHEKHOV

Chekhov (1860–1904), the grandson of a serf, was trained as a doctor but became a full-time writer of marvelous short stories; some are highly comic, others touching accounts of people's dreary lives. One of the best is "The Lady with a Dog," set in the resort of Yalta, where Chekhov, suffering from tuberculosis, lived for a time. Chekhov is best known for his great plays, such as *The Seagull* and *The Cherry Orchard*.

Sculpture of Chekhov and "The Lady with a Dog"

Scene from the 1965 film *Dr. Zhivago*

BORIS PASTERNAK

During the long period of Stalinist repression, Pasternak (1890–1960) translated Shakespeare and Goethe. He won the Nobel Prize for his novel about the Civil War, *Dr. Zhivago*. Published abroad in 1957, it caused anger in the Kremlin. Pasternak was expelled from the Soviet Writers' Union.

Mandelstam's satirical poem comparing Stalin to insects

The Cyrillic alphabet contains 33 letters

OSIP MANDELSTAM

Among Russia's remarkable writers of the early 1900s was the gifted poet Mandelstam (1891–1938), whose poems reflect great knowledge of the classical world. Banned from publishing in the 1930s, he was twice arrested and sent to concentration camps. He died in Siberia in 1938, his crime a satirical poem about Stalin.

LEO TOLSTOY

Tolstoy (1828–1910) was a great novelist who wrote highly acclaimed novels, among them the epic *War and Peace*, about Napoleon's invasion, and *Anna Karenina*, a tragic love story. He founded his own moral religion, based on Christianity, in which he rejected wealth. His ideas attracted followers from around the world, but he was attacked by the church and state. He died at a railway station, aged 82, having fled from home after family diputes.

ALEXANDER SOLZHENITSYN

Solzhenitsyn (b. 1918) was arrested at the end of World War II for criticizing Stalin. His experiences are reflected in *One Day in the Life of Ivan Denisovich*. Published in 1962, it was the first story about Soviet camp life to be printed.

Film still from *One Day in the Life of Ivan Denisovich* (1971)

Art and icons

IN ARCHITECTURE, PAINTING, and sculpture Russians throughout the ages have shown special feeling for color and shape. Religious art (icons, frescoes, and mosaics) dominated until the 17th century, when other subjects – portraits and landscapes – became popular. In the 19th century the Wanderers (a society of artists who portrayed the realities of life), led by Ilya Repin, painted ordinary people and scenes from Russian history. In the early 1900s, Mikhail Vrubel's unique style of painting influenced modern artists like Malevich, Kandinsky, and Chagall. At first vivid and daring, Soviet art was soon forced to portray positive images of Soviet life. Modern abstract art was forced underground but is free in the new Russia.

DISCOVERY OF BLACK GEORGE
Icons of St. George and the dragon were popular, but usually the horse was white, not black. This rare 14th-century icon was discovered in 1959 in a northern village near Arkhangelsk. It was being used as a shutter for a barn and was hidden by a thick layer of paint. The icon was spied as the shutter was being stripped for repainting. Moscow restorers carefully cleaned the shutter to reveal this delightful, well-preserved icon.

Pestle for grinding pigments to a fine powder

NATURAL PIGMENTS
Pigments (colors) used in icon painting are derived from the natural world. White comes from lead, black from ash. From clay comes ocher. Bright red is from vermilion, a mercury compound; gold occurs naturally.

HISTORY OF ICON PAINTING
In Byzantium, icons painted by formal rules were usually solemn and severe. But in Russia icon painting gradually took on a gentler, more emotional character. Andrei Rublev (c. 1360–1430) was one of the greatest Russian icon painters. He composed this beautiful picture, *The Old Testament Trinity*, of God the Father, Son, and Holy Ghost, in disguise, as guests of Abraham.

Bright blue lapis lazuli comes from silica rock

Red ocher

Gold

Vermilion (cinnabar)

Ground lapis lazuli

Icon restoration

Restoration of ancient icons is a painstakingly slow process. In the past, darkened icons were repainted – the new image on top of the old. In Soviet times restorers devised methods of preserving each layer.

Rublev's figures, bowed in thought, are painted in soft, luminous colors

Gold halo is a symbol of divine light

Faces and hands are often painted by specialist icon restorers

Icons are blackened over time by candle smoke

Glue is applied with a brush; a syringe may be used to inject glue into surface cracks

STRENGTHENING
Icon is strengthened by soaking with fish glue until supple. Glued transparent paper is then ironed onto surface to stick down any peeling paint and left for up to six months.

FINISHING TOUCHES
Finally, even with the old paint secure and clean, there are usually fragments where the image has entirely disappeared. To repaint these sections, some Russian icon restorers use watercolors and not the egg tempera paint of the original artists. They want future restorers to know from the type of paint where the icon has been restored, and where the original painting has survived.

Film is weighted down over ether to prevent evaporation

Ether is dabbed on to icon through material

CLEANING THE SURFACE
Glued paper is removed by wetting. After careful testing, the icon is cleaned with ether. It can take an hour or more to scrape away dirt from a small segment. Care is taken not to overlap a previously cleaned section. Oil and turpentine complete the cleaning.

Lighter sections have already been cleaned

Dirt is removed carefully with a sharp knife

BEGINNINGS OF REALISM
Ilya Repin (1844–1930) came from a peasant family; he painted not only portraits but also controversial political and historical scenes. His *Religious Procession in Kursk* shows the poverty and blind faith of the people, and the hostility of the mounted police.

SOVIET ART
By the 1930s artists had to obey the Communist Party policy that all art should reflect a positive view of Soviet life. Stalin and other Soviet leaders were portrayed as wise and kind by artists like Alexander Gerasimov (1881–1963). His namesake, Sergei Gerasimov (1885–1964), in his *Collective Farm Festivities* presents a false view of jolly life on the farm. It was painted in 1937, the worst year of the Great Terror, when hundreds of thousands, including farmers, were arrested.

Malevich used these shapes in textile and pottery designs during the 1920s

ABSTRACT ART
The burst of creativity in Russia in all the arts at the beginning of the 20th century was reflected in the appearance of a modern abstract art. The uneducated but immensely talented Kasimir Malevich (1878–1935) experimented with color and geometric shapes to suggest force, motion, and space.

Music and dance

THE BUFFOON
A most original and witty composer of the 20th century, Sergei Prokofiev (1891–1953) wrote vivid and exciting music for the ballet *Romeo and Juliet*. This brilliant scenery was for his comic 1915 ballet *The Buffoon*.

THE ORIGINS OF ST. PETERSBURG'S Kirov Ballet go back to the 18th century. In 1776, the Moscow Bolshoi ballet began, using orphan children as dancers. At the end of the 19th century, ballet choreographer Marius Petipa created *Sleeping Beauty* and *Swan Lake*, ballets written to music by Tchaikovsky, the first of many great Russian composers, including Stravinsky and Prokofiev, to write for the ballet. From 1909 on, Sergei Diaghilev, founder of the Ballets Russes, sponsored radical ballets that burst like bombshells onto the world. The best new ballets of the Soviet era include *Romeo and Juliet*, *Spartacus*, and *The Golden Age*. Pavlova, Nijinsky, Ulanova, and Nureyev are some of Russia's greatest dancers.

A SHOCKING COMPOSER
An original composer, Igor Stravinsky (1882–1971) shocked the public with his modern rhythms. He composed ballets for Diaghilev, such as the popular *Petrushka* (score sheet above). Stravinsky left Russia during World War I, but his work continued to be inspired by Russian folk music.

DIAGHILEV'S GENIUS
Sergei Diaghilev (1872–1929), manager of the Ballets Russes, attracted talented composers, choreographers, and artists, who together created outstanding ballets. He employed Mikhail Fokine as choreographer (creator of dance) to devise most of the company's famous ballets, including *Narcissus*. This brilliant costume for *Narcissus* was designed by Russian artist Léon Bakst, who excelled in the use of extravagant style and color.

"GOD OF DANCE"
After studying ballet, Vaslav Nijinsky (1889–1950) became a leading dancer of the Maryinsky Theater in St. Petersburg. Joining Diaghilev's Ballets Russes, he not only danced such roles as *Petrushka* but also choreographed daring ballets like *The Rite of Spring* and *The Afternoon of a Faun*. But Nijinsky's relationship with Diaghilev deteriorated and by 1917 he had grown paranoid and withdrawn. From 1918 on he spent his life in a mental hospital. His career had lasted just 10 years.

Nijinsky as Armida's page in *Le Pavillon d'Armide*

Pavlova dancing the Dying Swan

PRIMA BALLERINA
Anna Pavlova (1882–1931) was prima ballerina at St. Petersburg's Maryinsky Theater for several years before joining the Ballets Russes in 1909 and starring in Fokine's *Les Sylphides*. She finally left Russia during World War I and settled in London, where she formed her own small company. Pavlova was a superb classical ballerina with wonderful technique. She is shown here dancing in Tchaikovsky's *Swan Lake*.

REVOLUTIONARY BALLET

The *Rite of Spring* had music by Stravinsky, choreography by Nijinsky, and lyrics and costumes by the artist Nikolai Roerich. The wild drumming music was considered so outrageous at its first performance in Paris in 1913 that a near-riot broke out. The Paris performance, however, was followed by a successful London debut in the same year. *The Rite of Spring* is now considered a landmark in 20th-century ballet.

Cap by Roerich for a young man in The Rite of Spring

PAGAN RUSSIA

The subject of *The Rite of Spring* was pagan Russia before it became Christian. The ballet is divided into two parts: the first celebrates the adoration of the earth, while in the second, a chosen maiden dances herself to death as a sacrifice to the earth.

Squares, circles, waves, and dots are the basis of the design for the maiden's costume in The Rite of Spring

FOLK MUSIC

Russian folk music grew out of the pagan Slavs' ritual songs used in festivals and ceremonies. In medieval times people sang epic ballads, playing a one-string instrument, the *gusli*. Jesters entertained with comical songs and satires. Here, a 19th-century accordionist plays as peasants dance.

MUSICAL INSTRUMENTS

In early Russia the *domra*, a 3- or 4-stringed instrument with a rounded soundboard, and the *balalaika* with 3 strings and a triangular soundboard were popular. Among wind instruments the *rozhok* (shepherd's horn) and *dudka* (pipe) were played. The *balalaika* is still widely played, especially in villages and folk music bands.

The balalaika *normally has three strings and a fretted fingerboard*

The triangular soundboard is often painted with mythical figures

Crafts and traditions

IN THE PAST the isolation of Russian villages and the long, snowbound winters allowed peasants much free time to engage in craftwork. The abundance of wood encouraged carving; delightful wooden toys and domestic utensils, including the traditional drinking dippers (*kovsh*), were made in nearly every village. Some, like the colorful distaffs (*prialki*) for spinning, were brightly painted. Intricate embroidery and handmade lace are still produced in the northern towns. Icon painters, forbidden by the Bolsheviks in 1922 to pursue their craft, began to make lacquer boxes decorated with illustrations of fairy tales. Metal and pottery ware and clay figurines also have a long tradition.

SPINNING FLAX
Until recently, spinning and weaving took place in nearly every peasant home, and distaffs (*prialki*) were part of the essential household equipment. The women above, sitting on the porch of a large wooden house in northern Russia, are spinning flax using traditional distaffs.

COLORFUL EMBROIDERY
In medieval times, when Russian women were confined to the home, they occupied themselves by establishing workshops. Here they not only fashioned their family's clothes but also embroidered elaborate cloths and robes for church purposes. Humbler people decorated their linen towels, wall hangings, and dresses with embroidery or drawn-thread designs of ancient origin. The 19th-century linen towel (above) embroidered with red thread (*kumach*), comes from the Vologda region, north of Moscow.

WOODEN SPINNER
The distaff, made of pine or birch, is a long board with a base on which the spinner sits. The wool or flax is held by the round projections at the upper end and pulled by the spinner to make a thread. Distaffs are usually gaily painted with designs of flowers or animals – or, as here, the lion and the unicorn. It was common for a husband to present a distaff to his new bride.

Brightly painted distaff is carved out of pine

Seat for spinner, who holds the board in place with her weight

DIPPING DUCK
In medieval Russia, the handled dipper, *kovsh*, was commonly used as a bowl for holding drinks. Dippers made from precious metals were often presented to important people by the tsars. The ancient form of the dipper is based on the shape of a duck or the prow of a boat.

This painted wood dipper, carved with a duck's head and tail, was made in the early 19th century

Wooden dippers are mostly made from pine, but sometimes birch is used

Duck's head makes a useful handle to hold the bowllike dipper

Brocade embroidered with gold thread

Mother-of-pearl geese and flowers decorate the headdress

GINGERBREAD TREAT

In Russian villages, crisp gingerbread was customarily baked in carved wooden molds to celebrate weddings, funerals, and church holidays, and is still considered a great treat. The molds have a long history, but by 1800 traditional designs of animals, birds, and the flowering bush – a sign of rebirth – began to change as new patterns from news sheets, (*lubok,* p. 42), with their cartoonlike illustrations, became more widespread. This mold, made in the early part of the 19th century, depicts a bearded peasant dressed up for a festive occasion.

Ribbons were tied in a large bow at the back of the head

The water carrier is a favorite subject among clay modelers

The rooster is a popular figure in all types of Russian folk art

FESTIVE HEADDRESS

This beautiful bonnet, or*kokoshnik*, comes from northern European Russia, near Arkhangelsk. Made at the end of the 18th century, it is open at the back, which means it is for an unmarried girl: married women had to cover all their hair. Glass stones and mother-of-pearl are sewn on to a brocade background, which is stiffened with canvas. The headdress would have been worn for weddings and other important festivals, and was handed down from mother to daughter.

CLAY FIGURINES

Homemade clay figurines were once part of a pre-Christian magic ritual, but by the 19th century were used as toys. They are still made at Dymkovo, now part of the city of Kirov, on the Vyatka River. The toys are shaped from potter's clay mixed with river sand. They are then fired, whitened with chalk, and painted in strong colors. The craft, which was dying at the end of the 19th century, was revived during the Soviet period.

Bread and salt are offered on an embroidered towel

Salt is placed in a pot or in a dent on the top of the loaf

Pink silk ribbons stream out at the back

BREAD-AND-SALT GREETING

Russians traditionally greet important guests by offering bread and salt on an embroidered towel held by the hosts' youngest daughter. The guest breaks off a piece of bread, dips it in salt, and eats it. Salt was considered such a luxury in old Russia that it was stored in a strong warehouse in Moscow on the Solyanka, or Salt Street. Russians are very hospitable to this day, and welcome and offer food to guests, however unexpected.

Childhood

CHILDREN ARE WELL LOOKED AFTER in Russian society. Day care is provided for children whose parents work outside the home. Children start school at age 6 and finish by the age of 14 (16 if they continue their secondary education). Some schools still use Soviet school uniforms, which resemble those of tsarist times: girls wear brown dresses with white pinafores, boys wear blue tunics and trousers. Soviet children belonged to organizations that emphasized Communist ideals. Russia's children's literature and theater are among the best in the world.

BABY SWADDLING
It is customary in Russia to wrap babies up tightly in swaddling clothes for the first few months of life. Some people believe that this helps to straighten a baby's bones. Left swaddled for long periods of time, the babies are only occasionally unwrapped for a bath and a romp. Outside the hospitals, swaddling is gradually becoming less fashionable.

DRESSED LIKE MOTHER
This outfit from Orel province, southwest of Moscow, was typical of everyday wear for a little peasant girl in 19th-century Russia. It imitates her mother's clothes in that it consists of a jumper, or *sarafan*, with a long-sleeved blouse underneath. The printed cotton would have been bought in a store, but the outfit was sewn at home.

Strips of lace and other material decorate the dress

Felt boots are surprisingly waterproof on the ice

OUTDOOR GEAR
Children need to dress warmly in the cold Russian winter. This little boy, gliding down an ice slide, wears a warm coat, scarf, mittens, a fur-lined *shapka* cap with flaps to cover the forehead and ears, and felt boots, *valenki*, that are very warm in the snow.

WOODEN TOYS
Until the 20th century, Russian toys were made at home out of wood, the cheapest and most readily available material. Wood was made into puppets and all sorts of animals, from cows to bears. Colorful *matryoshka* nesting dolls were a favorite toy; now they are popular tourist souvenirs.

Matryoshka peasant dolls fit inside one another – the biggest one in the set holds the rest

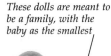

These dolls are meant to be a family, with the baby as the smallest

SUMMER CAMPS

During their three-month summer vacation, many Russian children enjoy the green countryside at a summer camp or country home (*dacha*). This is an important respite from the cities' crowded and noisy apartment complexes. Summer camps are organized through schools, or parents' employers, and are often held in the country houses of the former nobles.

COMMUNIST YOUTH GROUPS

Nearly all Soviet children between the ages of 7 and 10 belonged to the Octobrists; those ages 10 to 14 belonged to the Young Pioneers, while young people aged 14 to 28 joined the Komsomol (Young Communist League). These groups, which taught loyalty to the Communist Party, also provided hobby clubs the way Girl and Boy Scouts do. In the 1930s, however, Soviet brainwashing of children was so intense that some even betrayed their parents to the authorities. After 14-year-old Pavlik Morozov informed on his parents for helping kulaks (rich peasants), his father was shot. Pavlik was then murdered by his angry uncle, but became a Soviet hero.

The bear is a favorite character in Russian fairy tales

Girl Pioneers wore a blouse and skirt and, like the boys, red scarves

CHILDREN'S LITERATURE

Russia is rich in children's literature. Traditional fairy tales (*skazky*) were collected and vividly illustrated in the early 20th century. A famous character is the terrifying witch Baba Yaga, who has iron teeth and lives in a hut that stands on chicken's legs. Two recent children writers are Samuel Marshak, who wrote fairy tales, and Kornei Chukovsky, who wrote a Russian version of *Dr. Dolittle* called *Dr. Aibolit* ("Dr. Ouchithurts.")

SCHOOLS FOR THE GIFTED

The Soviets established special schools in the cities to encourage those talented in mathematics, languages, music, and sports. This little girl is studying dance in a ballet school. Only a few children get into the school; they have to show great talent. Along with learning ballet, they take the usual school courses.

National pastimes

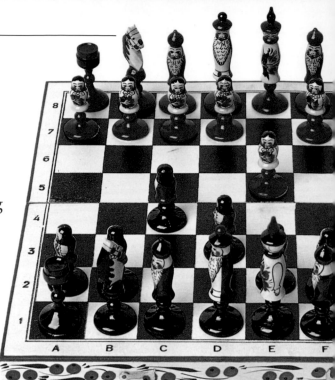

IN SUMMER RUSSIANS enjoy swimming, long walks in the countryside, and fishing. Winter activities include skating, cross-country skiing, and ice fishing. In autumn people of all ages love to go mushroom picking in the woods. Popular sports include soccer and ice hockey, at which Russia is a world leader. Tennis is rapidly becoming popular. Russians are also fond of gymnastics and perform well at many sports in the Olympics. Favorite games include chess and dominoes; older people can often be seen playing these in city parks. Even though most people have modern bathrooms, the weekly steam bath is still a regular custom in both the city and the countryside.

CHESS CHAMPIONS
The game of chess came to Russia from China 1,000 years ago. After the 1917 Revolution, chess was strongly encouraged, and clubs were organized in schools and factories. Many recent world champions have been Russian.

Buckets of this sort are used in steam baths for washing, or to throw water on the stove to create more steam

MUSHROOM PICKING
In the damp late summer and early autumn, thick clusters of mushrooms spring up in the woods and fields. Armed with baskets and buckets, people scour the countryside, and even city parks, for the many varieties of edible mushrooms. They take their trophies home to eat right away, or to dry for future use.

Birch twig bunches for beating dirt out of one's pores are sold at the entrances to steam baths

STEAM BATHS
Russians delight in their weekly steam bath (*banya*). Many villages have their own steam baths, while in the cities baths are found in every district. Friday and Saturday nights are the busiest, the traditional times for a good scrub. People steam their bodies to extreme temperatures, lash themselves with birch twigs (*venik*), then plunge into a cold bath or, if in the countryside in winter, roll in the snow.

COUNTRY REFUGE
In summer it is customary for city people to stay at a *dacha*, or country retreat. Children swim and play at the *dacha*, while adults fish, swim, tend the garden, walk in the woods, and enjoy a life in complete contrast to the bustle of the busy city.

Mushrooms are strung together, hung up, and dried in a warm kitchen; they last a long time

SLIPPERY SLOPES

In the deep cold of winter, ice slides can be made quickly on any slope, gentle or steep. Water poured down the slopes freezes rapidly. Children all over Russia enjoy such slides; some use sleds, but many just slither down in their thickly padded clothes (p. 52). Elaborate wooden slides like this one were built in places with few hills, such as St. Petersburg.

Chess is a popular game among children, who are usually encouraged to learn while still at school

Teapot rests conveniently on top for a quick refill of hot water when needed

TEA DRINKING

Russians love to drink weak black tea all day long. To have the tea readily available, they use a samovar ("self-boiling") urn. The water in this traditional samovar is heated by a central tube that is filled with pine cones and kindled by charcoal. The tea in the pot on top of the samovar can then be continually refreshed with the boiling water. Nowadays, samovars are usually heated by electricity.

Top opens here and pine cones are placed in the central tube

These wooden shutters keep out draughts during the long, harsh winters

A dacha *can be anything from a small wooden cottage to a sizable villa. Even a single room in a humble country cottage can be a* dacha

Screws attached these 1820s ice skates to warm boots

Ornate air vents provide an inlet for the oxygen needed to keep the pine cones alight

Fine samovars, such as this silver one, were made in the metal workshops of Tula, south of Moscow

Hot water to fill the teapot is obtained by turning the tap

ON FROZEN PONDS

Outdoor ice-skating has long been a national pastime in Russia for people of all ages. In winter, frozen ponds or flooded artificial rinks attract crowds of skaters who glide gracefully to piped music. The ice is regularly swept free of snow, and heated cabins allow skaters to put on their skates in comfort. These elegant skates belonged to Pavel Nakhimov, a famous Russian admiral, who in 1853 defeated the Turkish fleet during the Crimean War.

Annual festivals

THE IMPORTANT FESTIVALS of the year in Russia begin with New Year's, which is celebrated like the Western Christmas. Grandfather Frost and the Snow Maiden distribute presents, and on New Year's Eve families gather around a decorated fir tree for dinner and gift opening. Christmas is celebrated on January 7, because the Russian Orthodox Church follows the Julian calendar, which is 13 days behind the Gregorian calendar used elsewhere. Easter, the main religious festival of the year, remained popular, even in Soviet times. Military parades on May Day and the anniversary of the Revolution are no longer celebrated.

EASTER SERVICE
The service begins late on the eve of Easter and continues all night. At midnight the congregation, carrying lit candles, follows the priest around the outside of the church; this commemorates the women who came to the tomb of Christ and found it empty. At the doors of the church the priest proclaims, "Christ is risen." The worshipers joyfully reply, "He is risen indeed," and kiss their neighbors.

BREAKING THE FAST
As dawn breaks, the Easter service finishes, and the worshipers disperse to their homes to break their long fast with special Easter foods and colored eggs. The Easter cake (*kulich*), and the *paskha* (a sweet made of curd cheese) contain ingredients forbidden during Lent. Guests, who stop by all day, are offered the cakes.

Golden-domed monastery

On the side of the paskha *is a cross, or "XB," which stands for "Christ has risen"*

Men dress up in red robes and pass out pancakes to the crowds

PAINTED EGGS
In the week before Easter, everyone is busy painting eggs. Some are just boiled with onion skins, making lovely mottled brown and yellow colors. Others, with the yolk and white blown out through small pinholes in the end, are painted elaborately with religious or festive scenes. The eggs are eaten at the feast after the long Easter service.

This amusing painting shows a brown bear, one of Russia's national symbols, enjoying a sleigh ride

CELEBRATION OF LENT
The eve of Lent is traditionally the time of the butter festival, *maslenitsa*, when pancakes are eaten in large amounts. With snow still thick on the ground, some hardy people celebrate by breaking holes in frozen lakes and rivers and diving into the icy water.

MAY DAY FESTIVAL

In sympathy with the violent strike in Chicago on May 1, 1886, annual workers' demonstrations began in many countries, on May 1, 1890. In the Soviet Union (the workers' state) it was celebrated by large parades of workers carrying huge banners and portraits of political leaders. In the new Russia this festival has become an ordinary holiday.

"Long live the workers' festival"

This Orthodox church, complete with five onion domes, is carved out of ice

Athletes march through Red Square in the May Day parade of 1969

SOVIET PARADES

In the Soviet Union, military parades were held twice a year: on May Day (May 1), and on the anniversary of the Revolution (November 7, or October 25 by the old calendar). Soviet leaders stood on top of Lenin's mausoleum in order of rank to watch the military march through Red Square. Infantry tanks and giant rockets filed in awesome procession across the square, followed by gymnastic displays.

ICE FESTIVAL

The dead of a Russian winter is enlivened by a festival in which sculptures are carved out of ice; a competition is held for the best one. Russians have long enjoyed making ice buildings. In 1740 Empress Anna, known for her cruel jokes, ordered an ice palace built on the Neva River for the enforced marriage of her court jester.

Huge sculptures are built in city parks, and some can last until the start of the thaw in early spring

The new Russia

In August 1991 hardline Communists staged a coup (overthrow) against President Gorbachev and his reforms. The newly elected president of the Russian Republic, Boris Yeltsin, occupied the White House (Parliament building), in Moscow, and opposed the coup. Moscow citizens rallied behind Yeltsin and within three days the coup collapsed. At the end of 1991, the Soviet Union fell apart and the Russian Federation, led by Yeltsin, was born. In October 1993, Yeltsin dissolved the hardline parliament, which fiercely opposed his reforms. Again the parliament was occupied, this time by Communists and nationalists. Yeltsin used force; about 150 people died, but the hardliners were defeated. Since then, Russia has kept moving toward a market economy. Despite crime and corruption, life is improving for many people.

The Communist hammer and sickle flag came down on Christmas Day, 1991

NEW ECONOMY

In 1992 Russia attempted to change abruptly from a state-owned economy to a free-market system. At first there was confusion and huge price rises as the ruble (Russian currency) crashed in value. The economic reforms were then slowed down, and gradually the value of the ruble, which had never before operated in a free market, settled to about 5,000 to the U.S. dollar.

In 1912, a workman or shopkeeper would earn 500 rubles a year

In the 1990s, 500 rubles can only buy one egg

Cathedral of Christ the Savior was rebuilt in 1997 on its original site, where a swimming pool had stood since 1958

RESTORING THE PAST

Russian cities are taking on a fresh look as new businesses start and buildings are restored. Some important historic buildings destroyed during Soviet times – including the grand staircase of the Kremlin palaces, the Resurrection Gate on Red Square, and the Cathedral of Christ the Savior (p. 34) – have been rebuilt exactly as they were.

LAST LEADER OF THE SOVIET UNION

In 1985 Mikhail Gorbachev, the new Soviet leader, introduced a policy of openness (*glasnost*) followed by cautious reforms (*perestroika*). But he came under attack both by Communists opposing reform and radicals who wanted more democracy. After the failed coup of August 1991, Gorbachev was freed but found Yeltsin now in control and resigned four months later. But his reforms had made possible the new Russia.

OUT WITH THE OLD, IN WITH THE NEW

The four months from the August coup to December 31, 1991, were one of the most eventful periods in the history of Russia. In that time the Communist Party was dissolved, the republics that made up the Soviet Union broke away to form the loose grouping of the Commonwealth of Independent States (CIS), and Gorbachev, the last Soviet leader, resigned. On December 25, 1991, the red Soviet flag was lowered from the Kremlin. The new flag of Russia was raised in its place. The democratic Russian Federation was born.

New flag marked the end of Communism and the beginning of a democratic state

Estonia, Latvia, and Lithuania are collectively known as the Baltic States

The red, white, and blue tsarist flag is now the flag of the Russian Federation

Arctic Ocean

•Belarus

•Moldova   •Moscow

•Ukraine

Russian Federation

Republics of the Caucasus

Republics of Central Asia

Mongolia   China

POPULAR PRESIDENT

A construction engineer, Boris Yeltsin became Party boss in the Urals city of Sverdlovsk during the 1960s, and then of Moscow in the 1980s, under Gorbachev. Gorbachev fired him in 1987. Four years later, however, he became president of the Russian republic, the largest of the Soviet republics. Yeltsin was the first Russian leader in history to be popularly elected. In democratic elections in June 1996, Yeltsin, although unwell, was reelected president.

NEW RUSSIA

The Russian Federation, without the other 14 republics that made up the Soviet Union, is still the largest and potentially one of the most wealthy countries in the world. Of the 15 former Soviet republics, 12, including the Russian Federation, belong to the Commonwealth of Independent States (CIS). The Commonwealth's main aim is to promote economic and political cooperation between its members. The three remaining former Soviet republics – Lithuania, Latvia, and Estonia – have chosen not to join the Commonwealth of Independent States.

Index

Acknowledgments

Dorling Kindersley would like to thank:
Tamara Igumnova, Lyudmila Savchenko, Svetlana Zhizhina, Irina Poltusova, Tatiana Sizova, Yelena Smirnova, Yulia Gudovich, Lyudmila Dementieva, and Luiza Yefimova at the History Museum, Moscow; Pavel Rubinin of the Kapitza Museum, Moscow; Professor Roman Shatalov and Tatiana Susorova at the Polytechnic Museum, Moscow; Alexander Nikonov at the Museum of Armed Forces, Moscow; Tamara Shumnaya and Irina Orlova at the Museum of the Revolution, Moscow; Alexander Chepurnoi; Sergei Romaniuk; Yevgenia Grishina; Kate Cook; Zoya Yevgenyevna of Red Square Publications; Ella Piatigorsky; Joyce Roberson and Steven Platt of the Russian Orthodox Church; David Buckton at the British Museum; Cornelius & Son, London; Paul Cornish, Andy Hutcheson, and David Fearon at the Imperial War

Museum; The Britain-Russia Centre, London; The Earl of Pembroke and Trustees of the Wilton House Trust; and photographers Ian Jackson and Andy Brown.
Consultant: Geoffrey Murrell
Researcher: Robert Graham
Illustrator: John Woodcock
Modelmaker: Peter Griffiths
Index: Marion Dent
Jacket: Chris Branfield
Design and editorial assistance: Susila Baybars, Goldberry Broad, Maggie Tingle, Darren Troughton, and Jake Williamson
Picture credits:
The publisher would like to thank the following for their permission to reproduce their photographs:
a=above, c=centre, b=below, l=left, r=right, t=top:
AISA, Barcelona 22t, 23cb, 44c, 44b, 48bl;
Bridgeman Art Library: The Fine Art Society,

London 48 cr, Hermitage, St. Petersburg: Portrait Peter I (1723) Grigory Semyonovich 20bla, Portrait Catherine I (1729–96) Feodor Rokotov 20b, Kremlin Museums, Moscow 20cla, Lords Gallery, London 39c, Bibliotheque de L'Opera, Paris 48tl, Musee d'Orsay, Paris: Coronation of Nicholas II (1852–1929) Henri Gervex 24cl, Petit Palais, Geneva: Russian Peasants (1840–1940) Andreevich Malyavin 49cr, Private Collection 34-35b, State Russian Museum, St. Petersburg: Portrait of Rastrelli (1700–71) Pietro Rotari 28tr, Stapleton Collection 28ca, Tretyakov Gallery, Moscow: Tsar Ivan IV (1530–84) Vitor Mikhailovich 20cr, Religious Procession (1880–83) Ilya Efimovich Repin 47cbr; **e.t. archive:** 20c, 48cl; **Mary Evans Picture Library:** 9tr, 12bl, 16t, 17tl, 17bl, 19tl, 21br, 33br, 39tl, 45l, 48br; **Hulton Getty:** 8tl, 8b, 37t, 57; **Giraudon:** 23c, Lauros 19tr, 21cra; **The Ronald Grant Archive:** 43br, 45tr, 45b; **Robert Harding:** Paul van Riel 39cb; **Natural History Picture Agency:** Mirko Stelzner 11trb; **Michael Holford:** 14br; **The Hutchison Library:** 52cl,

55t, © Andzey 56t, 56br; **The Interior Archive:** 29tl; **Michael Jenner:** 28cl, 29cl, 36r, 37l; **David King Collection:** 14cl, 15cbr, 16cl, 20tl, 21tr, 30cl, 30bl, 30br, 31tl, 32cl, 33tl, 34cl, 35tl, 35cl, 35bl, 36t, 38tl, 38c, 42b, 43tl, 43tr, 46t, 47bl, 52tl, 53tl, 57tr, 58br; **Frank Lane Picture Agency:** 10tr; **Mander & Mitchenson:** 49tr, 49tr; **John Massey Stewart:** 28c, 29c; **Novosti Photo Library:** 15tr, 18cl, 23cl, 26-27cb, 30cb, 30-31b, 40cla, 40clb, 41cr, 41b, 47br, 50c, 53c; **Planet Earth Pictures:** William P. Paton 11b; **Nikolai Rakhmanonov:** 14t, 18tl, 21c, 24tl, 25tr, 25c; **Rex Features:** Sipa Press 58bl, 58b; **Ellen Rooney:** 18bl, 28-29b, 29tl, 29ca; **Oxford Scientific Films:** Martyn Colbeck 11cr, Mark Hamblin 11bra, Zig Leszczynski 10cl, Owen Newman 11trb; **Topham Picturepoint:** 24b; **Trip:** M. Jenkin 27tr, B. Turner 26-27ca, N&J Wiseman 37br; **Victoria & Albert Museum:** 49tl, 49l. Jacket: all DK special photography except **The Bridgeman Art Library:** back tr; **Giraudon:** front c; **Novosti Photo Library:** back bl; **Ellen Rooney:** front r; **Trip:** back br.

Above. The Arrest of Oscar Wilde
at the Cadogan Hotel. Poem by
Sir John Betjeman.
300 × 420 mm (11¾ × 16¾ in)
Dyed and stretch-mounted
vellum; gouache; steel pens.
Made in 1986 by Gerald Fleuss
and reproduced by kind
permission of Mr Leo Smith.

Calligraphy
Masterclass

Edited by Peter Halliday

THE CONTRIBUTORS

Thomas Ingmire
Richard Middleton
John Woodcock
Werner Schneider
Ethna Gallacher
Ewan Clayton
Brody Neuenschwander
Margaret Daubney
Lilly Lee Adamson
Gerald Fleuss
Susan Hufton
Sheila Waters
Tom Perkins
Gaynor Goffe
Peter Halliday

The Overlook Press
Woodstock, New York

First published in 1990 by
The Overlook Press
Lewis Hollow Road
Woodstock, New York 12498

Library of Congress Cataloging-in-Publication Data

Halliday, Peter ed.
    Calligraphy masterclass
    Includes bibliographical references
1. Calligraphy
                        I. Halliday, Peter, 1939-
Z43.C185   1990   89-71018
745.6'1—dc20   CIP

ISBN 0-87951-400-0

Distributed to the trade by Penguin USA

Produced and designed by
Savitri Books Ltd
Southbank House
Suite 106, Black Prince Road
London SE1 7SJ

Art direction and design by Mrinalini Srivastava
edited by Judith Warren

Typeset in Plantin by the Dorchester Typesetting Group Ltd
Reproduction by Landmark & Fotographics
Printed and bound in Spain by Sirven Grafic

Endpapers. Illuminated calligraphy on goatskin vellum. Close-up of *The Baite* by John Donne, written with quills, Chinese ink, watercolour and white gold. Peter Halliday (1980).

CONTENTS

INTRODUCTION

Calligraphy and Lettering: the Emergence of an Art Form

How does a calligrapher work? What makes the lettering artist use one form of letter in preference to another? What kind of aesthetic considerations are involved in interpreting subject matter as dissimilar as that which appears in this book? The work and commentaries presented here demonstrate the wide diversity of method and intention characteristic of today's calligraphy and fine lettering. The book is, I believe, unique in that, unlike so many of the books about calligraphy published recently, it sets out to show what goes into the making of modern calligraphy and lettering. Anyone with a serious interest in calligraphy will learn a great deal about the design process and what sets it in motion. The makers themselves discuss their motivation and methods, and describe in detail how their work was developed and brought to completion.

As a calligrapher with more than a passing interest in twentieth-century fine art, I have been fascinated to see how the calligraphers featured in this book are coming to terms with the changing relationship between art and craftsmanship. I was struck too, by their differing approaches; some contributors use words in extrovert and seemingly undisciplined ways, inviting us to share in their energy and exuberance, whereas the appeal of others lies in the sheer control and discipline of their letter formation. The edged pen has a spontaneous and irreversible effect on the letter being written; it impressed me to see each person coming to terms with this apparently limiting factor in so many different ways. Whether the lettering is engraved, painted, incised or drawn, the influence of traditional penmanship is fascinating to see. And throughout the book, the attention given to colour and decoration is very noticeable. Paradoxically, among all this diversity, I felt there to be an underlying unity, in the sense that here I believe we can see the emergence of an art form.

The late twentieth-century lettering arts movement, now well under way, has combined a sensitive awareness of tradition with a reassessment of that tradition's creative potential. Western letterforms have periodically been subject to reappraisal: in the eighth century the Holy Roman Emperor Charlemagne brought about a widespread revision of writing and manuscript production by encouraging the study and adaptation of the best letterforms from previous centuries. During the fifteenth century written letterforms from Charlemagne's time were adapted for the newly invented printing process. In the early twentieth century William Morris and his circle by laying emphasis on the relearning of medieval craft techniques and stressing the importance of the relationship between tools and materials in the hands of the maker, generated a revival of interest in all the arts and crafts but writing, illuminating and lettering in particular enjoyed a remarkable resurgence.

Two early masters of the English revival, Edward Johnston and his pupil Eric Gill, became very influential in the commercial world of type design as well as being significant forces in the sphere of fine hand-made lettering. They, along with others in Germany and the United States, rediscovered the importance of classical letter proportion; they arrived at an understanding of how lettering and writing developed and were used in historical manuscript production. Their work profoundly affected fields as diverse as penmanship and illumination, monumental and architectural lettering, type design and graphics, heraldry and signwork, and irreversibly changed the way lettering was regarded and practised.

Morris's craft ideals, particularly the notion that the use of machinery and mass-production techniques threatens the proper freedom and responsibility of the maker, have been questioned and subject to some reassessment throughout this century. Groups such as the Bauhaus rejected much of the 'handcraft' approach

6

which had developed in Britain and elsewhere. Most calligraphers in Britain, however, kept faith with the ideals which Johnston had inherited from Morris, and between the 1920s and 1950s tended to distance themselves from the commercial uses of lettering. They tried to ensure that calligraphy remained a craft activity and recreated manuscripts in the medieval tradition. The resulting work is, in terms of technique at least, among the most exquisite since the Middle Ages, while some of Edward Johnston's later work approaches the spirituality of oriental calligraphy. Yet the refusal of many scribes to reach across the widening gap between 'craft' and 'commercial' lettering meant that calligraphy in Britain became increasingly isolated. It remained almost untouched by the developments in graphic design which had revolutionized visual communication in the word as a whole. In Germany and, to some extent in the United States, calligraphers developed fruitful associations with typographers, graphic designers and architects.

Since the mid-1970s calligraphy has reached a previously unequalled level of popularity in the English-speaking world, which almost certainly exceeds the late nineteenth-century nostalgic interest in Gothic 'illumination'. That the present level of interest is popular, in the sense that a large number of people now study and take an interest in calligraphy, is made clear by the increasing sales of calligraphy pen sets and the proliferation of books on the subject. Exhibitions of calligraphy are always well attended. Notwithstanding this, much of the calligraphic work displayed is badly produced with little understanding of the intrinsic properties of letterforms. Many graphic designers remain suspicious about the commercial relevance of a craft-oriented activity. And there is a general lack of awareness of the proper qualities of calligraphy and fine lettering.

With the emergence of new directions in the lettering arts, there has inevitably been discussion and debate about whether calligraphy is to be regarded as art or craft. This question has often surfaced, but has not been fully resolved. The fine art world has never regarded calligraphy as being relevant to its own aesthetic criteria. After all, has any piece of calligraphy really confronted or disturbed us? It is possible for a piece of calligraphy to ask questions and confront issues; to act as a vehicle for the enhancing of thoughts, ideas and feelings? When faced with such questions, any debate about whether calligraphy is an art or a craft becomes less significant and we must find a way to the heart of the calligraphic process. Painters have to master the actual craft of painting before their work can speak for itself and likewise calligraphers must be the consummate masters of many techniques before a piece can convey its purpose. Unlike painters, calligraphers need to confront the words as well as the overall purpose, or intention, of the work. This inevitably constitutes a constraint and a challenge. The resulting process is not unlike the composer setting words to music. The calligrapher becomes both composer and performer, with the performance permanently before us.

In the process of interpretation calligraphers run the risk of devaluing the great literature, or the profound words whose meaning they are attempting to realize and communicate. They must therefore think deeply about and feel profoundly for those words if they are not to trivialize the very substance of the work. Perhaps the greatest temptation is to allow the work to become dominated by skill and the words to be overwhelmed by technique. Although calligraphers are likely to be concerned with methods and techniques, in the mind and hand of a master these will almost inevitably be subordinated to the concept of the work: used, not as ends in themselves, but as the means through which the substance is sought and communicated. Some contemporary calligraphy addresses this important issue squarely; but more often it seems to be put on one side and not seen as a main consideration. Until calligraphers confront this difficulty more consistently, the seriousness of calligraphy as an interpretive art must remain under suspicion.

Calligraphy can be approached in many different ways – calligraphers need not worry about being 'artists' or 'craftsmen' but simply delight in the beautiful

and sensual shapes of letterforms for their own sake. If they are to combine technique and skill as the means to effective communication, however, calligraphers, like graphic designers, must use their ability to choose, adapt and invent letterforms and designs to meet particular needs. It is no mere coincidence that some of the greatest type designers of this century have acquired their understanding of letters as calligraphers and have thereby had a profound effect on the appreciation of lettering, type and printing.

The exponents of contemporary calligraphy may have their roots in the craft traditions of the past on which they depend for technical excellence but they are reaching out towards a future which is uncertain, exciting and adventurous. This book displays the work of people who care profoundly about the words they use, and consider with respect how these are interpreted, be they simple inscriptions, titles or timeless literature.

Peter Halliday, November 1989

Stage 1 of Thomas Ingmire's piece.

THOMAS INGMIRE

Studio: 845 Lombard, San Francisco, California 94133, USA, tel: 415-6734938
Born in USA in 1942
Fellow of the Society of Scribes and Illuminators since 1977

Calligraphic training: studied with Donald Jackson in 1977 and undertook independent calligraphic study at Newberry Library, Chicago in 1980. Has taught workshops and given private classes throughout North America and England since 1977

Recent commissions: Richard Harrison; Joseph Goldyne; many private commissions and work held in numerous major collections

Main publications: 'Notes on Techniques', *Painting for Calligraphers*, Marie Angel; recent work is reproduced in *Lettering Artists of the 80's; Modern Scribes and Lettering Artists II; Words of Risk – the art of Thomas Ingmire*, Michael Gullick

Recent exhibitions: Denenberg Fine Arts, San Francisco; Pence Gallery, Davis; Jacksonville Art Museum; The Master Eagle Gallery, New York; San Francisco Public Library; Markings Gallery, Berkeley

Calligraphic Panel

'Everything is For Sale' was developed at a time when I was doing research into the theories and working methods of artists from the American Abstract period. The inspiration came from comments by Adolph Gottlieb, an important artist from this period. (In the 1950s A. Gottlieb developed what he called 'pictographs' – panels divided into chequerboard compartments and later into bands containing Red Indian magic symbols.) He stated that he often began a painting by arbitrarily dividing a page into five parts. As an experiment I decided to begin a piece in the same way, though as it turned out, and for no particular reason, the division was into four rather than five parts. Each division was demarcated by a line of blue versal capital letters. At this stage the words were taken from a translation of a series of poems about cities by Arthur Rimbaud, another arbitrary decision, although I had recently completed a piece titled 'The City', which used those texts.

Stage 1, shown on the left is already a considerable development from the initial lay-outs. The blue lines of versals remain and I used the large letters A, B, C, D, E to divide the vertical panel on the right into smaller shapes. The division of the design into sections, as well as the inclusion of the number '13' and of the red circular burst near the centre of the page were influenced by Gottlieb's work – many of his 'pictographs' incorporated primitive marks and symbols. The red and pale yellow areas were made by spreading gouache paint onto the page with pieces of cut card.

At this point the work had also undergone a number of 'washings' – a process which involves allowing water to run over the page to remove and disperse some of the colour. I added the fine white 'scribble' writing and included more gouache colour between washings. Finally, the work was mounted using wheat starch onto another sheet of paper, Arches text, which recreated a smooth, flat working surface and gave additional support to the original paper.

9

Stage 2

All the work on this piece was spontaneous, done without the aid of any tracing – the working process can best be described as 'responsive', involving techniques of adding to and subtracting from the page. In **stage 2**, I attempted to create a new overall page structure, as I felt that the original divisions lacked any form of unity or harmony. I used diluted white acrylic gesso, spread with a piece of cardboard, and patterns of white 'scribble' writing to obscure the existing divisions. The 'burst' image, previously a focal point, was obliterated by spraying the page with water and lifting some of the colour with a sponge. The piece at this stage seemed gaudy and excessive, reminiscent of the theme of a Rimbaud poem, titled 'Sale'.

Stage 3 represents a further attempt to alter the page structure. The line 'Everything is for sale' from the Rimbaud poem was written across the top as a means of unifying the page. Other phrases from the poem as well as some of my own words were added to reinfore some of the diagonals established in the previous stage. However, I was unhappy with the convergence of the five diagonals in the upper left-hand part of the page. This established another focal point, which seemed to compete with the rhythms of shape and line active within the rest of the page. The broad, almost transparent white vertical band, from top to bottom along the left-hand side of the page was made as a means of altering the impact of those converging diagonals. The white band was created by applying a dilute mixture of acrylic gesso with a soft brush.

Stage 3

Stage 4

The finished piece. (Left)
Calligraphic panel, 'Everything is
for Sale' (1987)
584 × 305 mm (23 × 12 in)
Edmonds paper adhered to Arches
text; acrylic gesso and gouache;
cut card, watercolour brushes,
pointed metal pens and quills.

Stage 4 (*see* previous page) shows a detail of the left-hand panel. After
creating the white band, I felt that its texture needed to be enriched. I also
wanted to present the text in a more readable form. In the final analysis,
however, the page did not work as one unified whole, but rather as two
separate parts.

For the final completed work (*See* picture on opposite page), I discarded the
panel on the left and the large blue letters at the top. Some of the letters which
had been pushed into the background by the washing process were repainted
to pull them forward. The rhythmic play of movement between foreground
and background, the fragmented phrases, textured background writing and
harsh 'hot' colours were an attempt to express the rawness, complexity and
passion of the modern urban world.

Manuscript Book

Alchimie du Verbe was a manuscript book commissioned in 1984 by Richard
Harrison. The choice of text was left to me and I decided to use part of *Une
Saison en Enfer*, a prose poem in nine fragments by Arthur Rimbaud.

I did sporadic research over a three year period before I began actual work
on the book. During this phase I was particularly interested in defining the
theme and mood of each poem and prose section of the text. The prose text
which leads into the double page spread shown on pages 18 and 19 of this
book, begins: 'I got used to elementary hallucination . . .' and continues by
describing a variety of vivid images of madness and suffering. A series of
etchings by Jim Dine (**1**) was the inspiration for this page and its later
development. The pencil sketch (**2**) is an early study which incorporates a
fairly close representation of Dine's etching.

1. Part of Jim Dine's etching, the
starting point for the page.

2. Early pencil sketch.

13

I then worked on draft pages for the entire book, executed at full scale over double page spreads, and using black ink on a good quality paper. I folded enough pages to comprise the entire book and worked through the text sequentially from beginning to end. Throughout I tried to use lettering to express visually the various moods of the text. The image from the Dine etching became the focal point for the crazed, exploding page shown in (**3**).

3. The page incorporating Rimbaud's words and my interpretation of Jim Dine's etching.

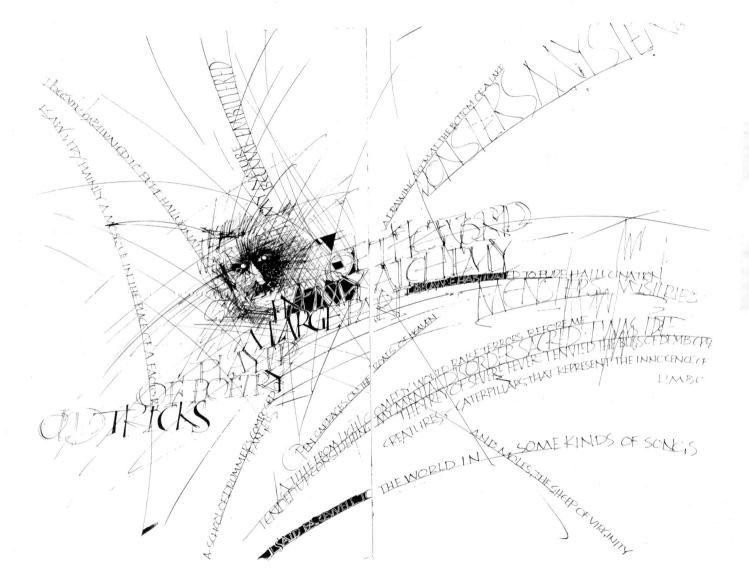

A series of small sketches (**4**) was developed as a means of assessing the visual rhythm of various images and the sequence in which they fell; they helped me place each spread within the context of the book as a whole. These sketches led to a number of decisions – to use both the French text and the

4. Plan of the page sequence within the book.

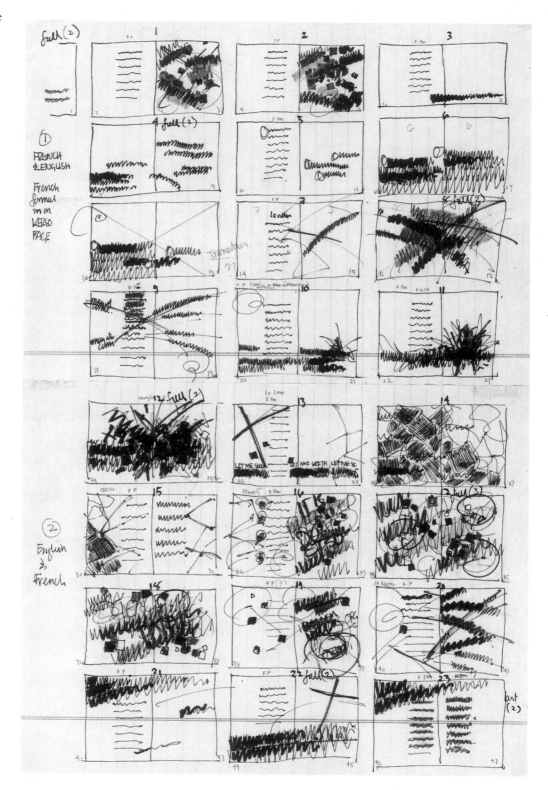

English translation and to write the French formally in columns, so that it would serve as an anchor for the English text, which would be written more expressively. One column of French text was included on each double page spread, the position of this column differing throughout the book.

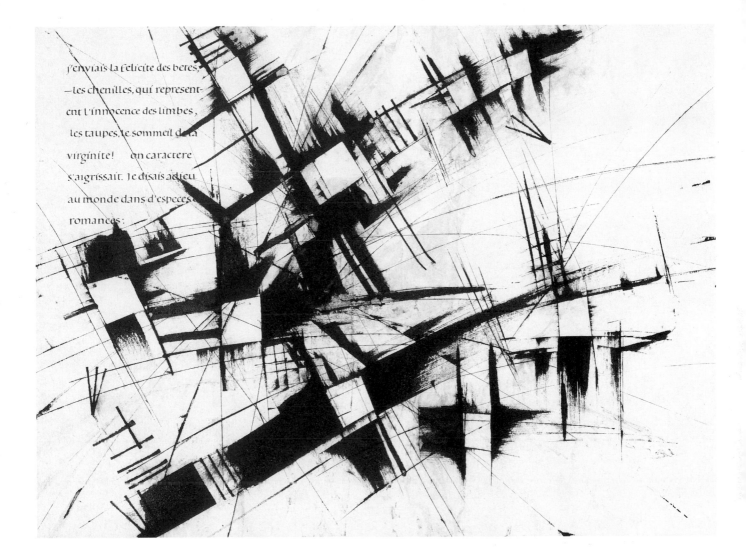

Within the image:

j'enviais la félicité des bêtes,
—les chenilles, qui represent-
ent l'innocence des limbes,
les taupes, le sommeil de la
virginité!   on caractere
s'aigrissait. Je disais adieu
au monde dans d'especes
romances:

5. Final draft study of work
shown on pages 18 and 19.

The picture above (**5**) shows a final draft study, which was executed on the same paper, Edmonds, as I used in the finished book. After I had written the French text I made broad marks with cardboard and the fine lines were done with edged metal poster pens. The page was then run under water to spread the ink, creating an ethereal, smokey background. This draft page was done primarily to gain confidence with the mark-making and washing technique.

The picture on the right (**6**) shows a page in progress out of the final book. The differences between the final page and the final draft study reflect my approach to the working process. I felt that it was important to keep the image spontaneous and therefore made no attempt to duplicate exactly what was created in the final study.

A number of stages leading to the completion of this particular spread (*see* picture below and finished page overleaf) are not shown here. First I used a ruling pen to put down lines of gum ammoniac as a base for the gold leaf which frames the miniature-like images. Next, 24 carat gold leaf was applied. Finally the pictures themselves were sketched onto the paper with pencil, and then painted using watercolours and gouache.

6. Final page in progress.

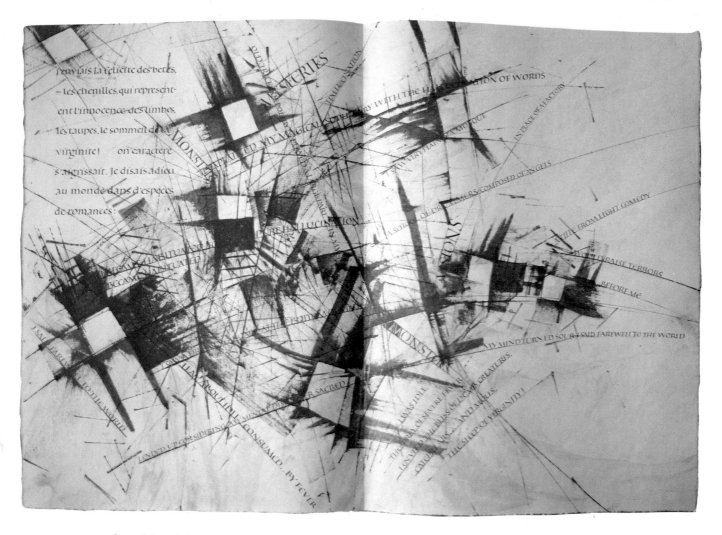

One of the miniatures incorporated in the finished spread.

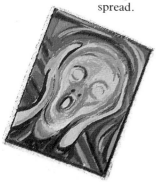

The miniatures incorporated in the piece, (*see* finished page overleaf) all of which depict a kind of horror, are an odd collection from various sources. Some are derived from illuminated manuscripts while others were inspired by details from paintings by famous modern artists, including Salvador Dali, Francis Bacon and Edvard Munch. The works of surrealist artists have a connection with Rimbaud, as some critics consider that Rimbaud's life and poetry served as an important aesthetic doctrine for many of the surrealist painters and poets.

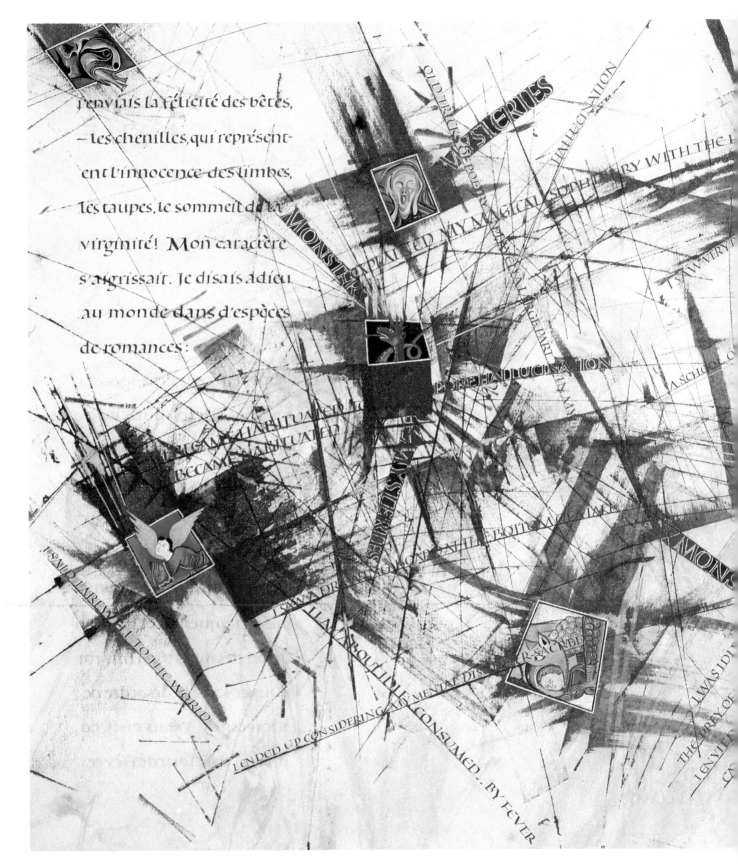

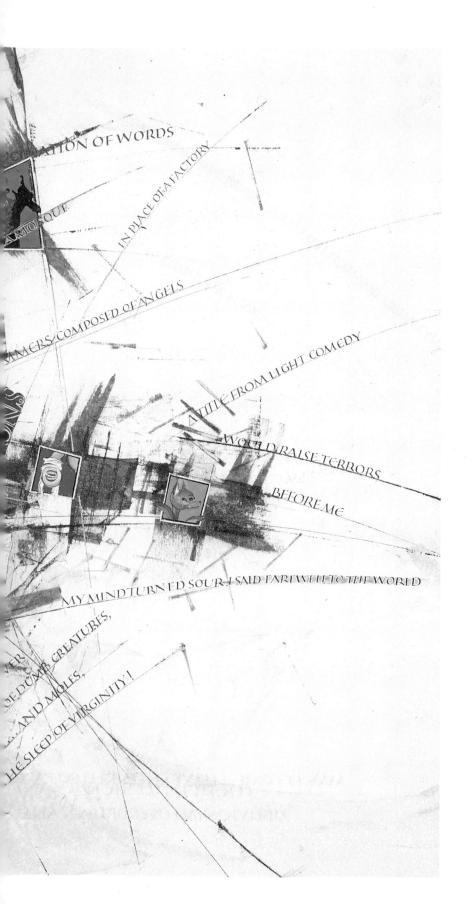

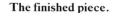

The finished piece.
Double page spread from manuscript book: 'Alchimie du Verbe' (1988)
309 × 221 mm (12 × 8¾ in)
Edmonds paper; Sumi ink, stick ink, gold leaf over gesso and gum ammoniac, shell gold, powdered pigments bound with gum arabic and gouache, cut card, watercolour brushes, automatic pens, metal pens and quills. The book was bound by Eleanore Ramsey.

Two of the miniatures included in the finished spread.

RICHARD MIDDLETON

Author's photograph by Alan Ginman

Studio: 16 Ringwood Crescent, Nottingham, NG8 1HP, tel: 0602-289028
Born in Australia in 1957
Fellow of the Society of Scribes and Illuminators since 1988; member of Letter Exchange since 1989

Calligraphic training: Digby Stuart College, Roehampton Institute (1984-88) under Ann Camp, Tom Perkins, Gaynor Goffe and Gerald Fleuss. Has taught workshops throughout the UK

Recent commissions: the Diocese of Southwell; Fisons plc; Intermediate Technology; Souvenir Press; Survival International; numerous private commissions of original calligraphy and also for reproduction

Main publications: 'The Geometry of the Foundational Hand', *The Scribe*, no. 38, 1986

Recent exhibitions: SSI exhibitions 1986-89; Rufford Craft Centre; Paperpoint, London

Contemporary expressionist calligraphy draws attention through craftsmanship to words the calligrapher wishes to echo. A quote may be absurd, profound, controversial, ambiguous, or simply funny, but it must be worth the effort of writing. Since the most profound human thought is often religious, and the most concise statements are often expressed through poetry, this frequently determines the choice of texts.

Panel with Religious Text

This particular piece developed over three years and was written out a total of thirty-four times, the later versions entailing only quite small adjustments of a preceding copy. Initially, all I had decided on was the quote from Don Cupitt's book *The Sea of Faith*, but by the second version (**1**) the cross of Christianity and the mandala of Buddhism had become part of the design. Italic was selected as I felt it best reflected the adventurous theology of the writer's words.

One of my aims was to create tension by contrasting Cupitt's questioning, adventurous spirituality with the dull unthinking orthodoxy of obedience to the Church's teaching, and a few versions later (**2**) the Creed was included as a contrast with the original quote. Both are non-Biblical, and both start with the words 'I believe'. Without this tension, calligraphy could be accused of being nothing more than an elegant advertisement for other people's writings. The Creed was written in Latin to emphasize its traditional dogmatism, and in a Roman hand because it is in Latin. Originally I intended to write it in black on white to reflect its uncompromising interpretation by many Christians. This had to be modified to grey on white because the black would have been too 'heavy' for the blue which I had chosen to echo the spirituality of Cupitt. Green was introduced to suggest growth through the cross and mandala. Several greens were mixed so that, in the final version, the shade of green matched the shade of blue used in the writing.

20

I decided to discard this attempt: the lay-out does not work as the Latin can't easily be read.

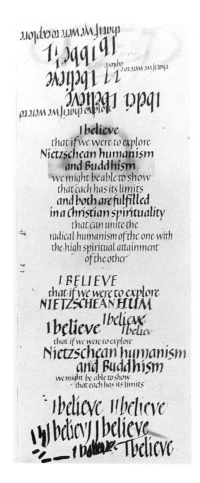

1. The quote by Don Cupitt which was the starting point for this piece. By then the rough already included the joint emblems of the cross and the mandala of Buddhism.

2. This rough was my fifth attempt at resolving the piece. The Latin words of the Creed appear in grey 'around' the central core of the piece which is the Cupitt quote and the cross/mandala symbols. The lines of the Latin text are broken up to fit around the central block which makes them difficult to read. Clearly a radically different approach was called for.

Picture **3** (*overleaf*) shows a development in which the Latin Creed is interspersed with the Cupitt words. All work is to some extent experimental: this was an experiment that did not quite work, for the whole thing was now too fragmented. I felt that the stability could be improved by having a central channel of white as a focus, and that the airbrushed emblem, now too stark, needed somehow to be better integrated with the writing.

21

I BELIEVE that if we were to explore

Credo in unum deum, patrem
omnipotentem, factorem coeli et terrae,
Deo vero visibilium et invisibilium.
Et in unum dominum Iesum Christum,
Deum verum de filium dei unigenitum.
Et ex patre natum ante omnia saecula.
Deum de Deo, lumen de lumine,

Nietzschean humanism & Buddhism

we might be able to show that each has its limits and both are fulfilled

Genitum, non factum, consubstantialem
patri: per quem omnia facta sunt.
Qui propter nos homines, et propter
nostram salutem descendit de coelis.
Et incarnatus est de Spiritu Sancto
ex Maria Virgine: et homo facto est.

Crucifixus etiam pro nobis sub Pontio Pilato:
passus et sepultus est. Et resurrexit tertia die,
secundum scripturas. Et ascendit in coelum:
ussedet ad dexteram Dei Patris. Et iterum ventur
est cum gloria judicare vivos et mortuos:

in a Christian spirituality

that can unite the radical humanism of the one

cujus regni non erit finis. Et in spiritum
sanctum Dominum et vivificantem:
qui ex Patre, Filioque procedit. Qui
cum Patre, et Filio simul adoratur
et conglorificatur, qui locutus est

per prophetas. Et unam, sanctam,
catholicam et apostolicam Ecclesiam.
Confiteor unum baptisma in
remissionem peccatorum. Et expecto
resurrectionem mortuorum.
Et vitam venturi saeculi. Amen.

with the high spiritual attainment of the other

3. In this later development I tried to juxtapose sections of the Latin Creed with sections of the Cupitt quote. I was still not happy: the text appears fragmented and seemed to bunch towards the centre of the piece.

One of the paste-ups used to find the right amount of white space between sections is illustrated here (**4**). It is generally considered best, theoretically, to try several variations before pasting down the one that works best as a final lay-out. Unfortunately, the cut edges of paper produce lines which, though barely visible, affect the appearance of the white spaces, and I find that a final rough needs to be written on a single piece of paper.

The upside-down writing on the left-hand side was done to establish the line lengths needed to leave a clear central channel. For the finished work, tiny pencil marks were traced onto the left-hand side to mark the beginning of each word so that any adjustment of the writing could be made all along the

line, and not result in 'bunching' at the end of the line. There is an inevitable loss of freedom in those lines of writing, a compromise I had to make for the sake of the lay-out.

I BELIEVE that if we were to explore

Nietzschean humanism & Buddhism

we might be able to show that each has its limits, and both

are fulfilled in a Christian Spirituality

that can unite the radical humanism of the one with the high spiritual attainment of the other

4. By this stage I had decided to introduce a channel of white space running down the central section of the piece. To establish the required line lengths for the left-hand section of the piece, I pasted sections of text upside down so that the lines are ranged flush along the central white channel and start unevenly from the left.

For the final version, as used in my Fellowship show of 1988 (*see* page 24), it had seemed appropriate to try a hand-made Indian paper, and on this the gouaches wrote beautifully without any sandarac, even where the airbrush had sprayed. The bits of straw in the paper allowed the sprayed area to merge into the background, and where the lumpiness of the paper occasionally intruded into a letterstroke (e.g. the second 'd' in 'Buddhism'), it lent a vitality to the writing. The width of the paper was only just enough to accommodate all the writing; I had to leave the curved sides uncut, because cutting them straight would have reduced the margins too much. The top margin was too wide, and so that the edge of the paper would not appear harsh against the other three deckled edges, it was carefully torn along a dampened crease. The three curved edges meant that the piece had to be put on a mount which could then be cut square for the framing. The colours of both mount and frame were chosen to harmonize with the dominant blue writing.

I decided to have the cross on the left-hand side where it would be 'read' first because Cupitt is primarily a Christian theologian, but the areas occupied by the cross and mandala symbols were calculated to be geometrically equal so that they balance each other.

The acknowledgement line at the bottom was written in dark blue to tie up with the 'I believe' at the top, and referred not only to the book, but to the chapter, so that the quote could be found readily and examined in context by anyone wishing to look it up.

The balance of this piece was affected by very small adjustments in the lay-out, two of which illustrate this point. Half-way down the left-hand side it was necessary, even using an ampersand, to have one long line intruding upon

I BELIEVE THAT IF WE WERE TO EXPLORE

Credo in unum Deum, Patrem
omnipotentem, factorem coeli et terrae,
visibilium omnium et invisibilium.
Et in unum Dominum Jesum Christum
Filium Dei unigenitum. Et ex Patre natum
ante omnia saecula. Deum de Deo, lumen
de lumine, Deum verum de Deo vero.

Nietzschean humanism, and Buddhism

we might be able to show that each has its limits, & both

are fulfilled in a Christian spirituality

Genitum, non factum, consubstantialem Patri:
per quem omnia facta sunt. Qui propter
nos homines, et propter nostram salutem
descendit de coelis. Et incarnatus est de
Spiritu Sancto ex Maria Virgine: et homo factus est.

Crucifixus etiam pro nobis sub Pontio Pilato:
passus, et sepultus est. Et resurrexit tertia die,
secundum scripturas. Et ascendit in coelum:
sedet ad dexteram Dei Patris. Et iterum
venturus est cum gloria judicare vivos
et mortuos: cujus regni non erit finis.

Et in Spiritum Sanctum Dominum et vivificantem,
qui ex Patre Filioque procedit. Qui cum Patre,
et Filio simul adoratur et conglorificatur:
qui locutus est per Prophetas. Et unam,
sanctam catholicam et apostolicam Ecclesiam.
Confiteor unum baptisma in remissionem
peccatorum. Et expecto resurrectionem
mortuorum: et vitam venturi saeculi. Amen.

that can unite the radical humanism of the one with the high spiritual attainment of the other

FROM CHAPTER NINE, THE SEA OF FAITH, BY DON CUPITT, DEAN OF EMMANUEL COLLEGE, CAMBRIDGE

The finished piece.
Panel with religious text. (1988)
820 × 670 mm (32¼ × 26¼ in)
Hand-made Indian paper;
gouache; steel pens; airbrush.

the margin: 'that each has its limits, & both'. The only way I could prevent the piece being slightly weighted to the left, was by writing a similarly long line in the small grey writing on the other side: '*Spiritu Sancto ex Maria Virgine: et homo factus est*'. Exactly the opposite thing happened at the bottom of the piece. The last line of blue writing, 'attainment of the other', gives a heavy and definite lower border, but because the grey writing on its left is so much lighter in visual impact, I had to make that final grey line a little below the level of the blue so that they both had the same *perceived* position.

All the writing was done with Winsor and Newton designers' gouaches. These did not come in the exact colours I needed, so each of the three colours used was very carefully mixed. I squeezed half an inch of the darkest colour out of the tube into a palette, and added half-inch measures of the lighter colours, keeping a written record of the amounts included. Every new half-inch was thoroughly mixed in with a paintbrush to check the colour. When the mixture seemed right, I tested it by making a small brushmark on the paper to be used for the finished piece, because colours often change slightly as they dry. Then I scraped all the mixture out into a photographic film canister which, having a relatively small exposed surface area, does not dry out rapidly as paint in a palette does. I mixed in distilled water (tapwater can contain chemicals which may affect the paint) until the gouache had the consistency of milk, and added a drop of Winsor and Newton gum arabic for every 6 cubic centimetres (large teaspoonful) of water to help glue the paint onto the paper. Too much gum seems to make the writing blobby. For sharpest writing, a lot of water is best but if there is too much water the letters dry translucent.

It is important to stir the paint thoroughly every time the pen is refilled, because the colours may settle out in the canister. Indeed, the colours in the large writing of this piece started to separate in the freshly written letterstrokes, and to prevent uneven drying, after I had written each line I mopped up the excess paint from every letterstroke with a twisted corner of tissue paper.

For the airbrushing, it was not important to use colours that wrote well, and provided I used permanent, light-fast colours any mixture that gave me the right colour would have done. In fact, the mixture I used was greatly diluted, and to avoid wetting the paper unduly which would have cockled it, the sprays were done very lightly, with long periods between applications.

Although I prefer to work with very wet quills, the paper I was using did not respond well to them and the whole of this piece was written with metal pens. 'I believe' was written with an Automatic (Boxall) pen. The first section of the Latin Creed was written with a William Mitchell no. 3 nib ground to a right-hand oblique angle. All the other writing was done with different sizes of Brause nibs with the reservoirs removed. I dislike the stiff feel that the fitted reservoirs give to Brause nibs, and I find the slip-on reservoirs supplied with the Mitchell nibs never quite fit, and are of metal too thick to be bent easily to shape. Instead, I make my own 'overhead' reservoirs based on the Brause design, using paper-thin shim brass which I rescued from a deceased electric blanket. This can be cut with scissors, folds without difficulty, yet has enough strength to retain its shape (**6**).

6. My own version of an overhead reservoir made of shim brass.

With the larger pen sizes I cover the whole nib end with gouache, but with the smaller nib sizes I find I get a sharper letterstroke by filling just the reservoir, so that the only gouache getting to the writing edge of the pen is by capillary flow down the slit of the nib. After writing, I clean the nib and reservoir with a toothbrush, generally somebody else's.

The airbrush used was a small, inexpensive Badger model. The masks were cut from Frisk Masking Film, the stickiness of which was reduced by adhering it to successive pieces of paper until it would only just stay attached. This prevented fibres of the paper lifting as it was peeled off, which would have damaged the writing surface. The paper was hung vertically and sprayed from a distance of about a foot, the airbrush being checked immediately before each spraying on an adjacent piece of newsprint to make sure it would not spit and ruin the sheet.

I use a B pencil sufficiently sharp to cause pain if carelessly handled, honing it to a point on a piece of wet-and-dry. Because of the paint sprayed on by the airbrush, the ruling could not be erased. Accordingly, each line of writing in the final rough was carefully measured and the pencil lines made exactly that length. I prefer to leave pencil lines anyway: they are part of the construction, like visible joints in a piece of fine woodwork, or flying buttresses outside a cathedral.

Finally, the paper had to be torn to size. Handmade paper does not have a grain direction, and cannot easily be torn in straight lines. To get a straight tear along the top, it was first folded sharply along a straightedge with a bone folder. Water was then applied carefully to the fold with a fine paintbrush to weaken it locally, and when the crease was thoroughly wet, the paper was slowly pulled apart with the fingers.

To complete a complex piece of work like this, one needs to feel sufficiently positive about one's own ideas to keep going, even though it seems that every rough is a failure. To be open to suggestions and advice from other people can also help. This panel started as a student piece done while I was at Digby Stuart College, and many of my decisions were influenced not only by the tutors' comments, but also by observations made by other students. An advantage of having a number of critics is that the advice received is frequently in conflict, and in the end the responsibility for all decisions was, as it should be, my own.

Commissioned Book

I was commissioned by the Intermediate Technology Development Group Ltd to write each year the names of their Associates in a leather-bound book. The significance attached to the names suggested large, bold writing, and I chose a modified foundational hand as being suitable for a dignified, formal book. The size of writing in turn dictated a large, bold binding, and I suggested that it should be possible to create a book to which pages could be added each year. Intermediate Technology agreed to let me design a binding specifically for this purpose.

Two oak boards were made which, with quarter circle mating edges, would roll open onto the exposed, Japanese-sewn spine of the pages. Vellum-reinforced endpapers were sewn to the wooden boards to give them stability when being handled. These boards were secured to each other by a stout, interlacing cord threaded through slots cut in the inner margins of the pages.

The exposed spine of the book meant that it was necessary to make a protective box, of matching oak. Each year the new pages are removed from

Above. The book I was commissioned to produce by Intermediate Technology Development Group Ltd.

beneath the false bottom of the box, so that as the book grows thicker the false bottom sinks, giving a constant snug fit. The new Associates are written in. Then the padouk slats are tapped out of the oak boards to expose the cord binding, which is untied and unthreaded. The Japanese sewing is cut, the new pages inserted and the spine is resewn. The cord is replaced through the boards, retied, and the padouk slats tapped back into place.

Right. The book in its oak boards binding. The padouk slat is halfway out, revealing the cord binding.

The finished piece.
Commissioned book. (1988)
Page size 388 × 255 mm
(15¼ × 10 in)
Binding designed by the scribe
who was taught bookbinding by
Jen Lindsay FDB.
Woodwork by Christopher
Palfrey.
BFK Rives printmaking paper;
stick ink; watercolour, gouache;
raised and burnished gold.
Reproduced by kind permission of
Intermediate Technology
Development Group Ltd.

JOHN WOODCOCK

Studio: 1 Stanley's Cottages, Dene St, Dorking, Surrey RH4 2DW, tel: 0306-889107

Born in England in 1924

Fellow of the Society of Scribes and Illuminators since the 1950s; member of the Corporate Society of Designers since the 1960s

Calligraphic training: Royal College of Art (1946-50) under Dorothy Mahoney and Irene Wellington. Taught in Department of Graphic Design at St Martin's School of Art, 1965-87; part-time teaching at many colleges, including Digby Stuart. Has taught workshops in USA 1985-87.

Recent commissions: Redesigned certificates for the Royal Academy School, The Museum Association and the Royal Pharmaceutical Society of Great Britain. Redesigned SSI Journal in summer 1985. Numerous commissions, often for print/publishing.

Main publications: *Binding Your Own Books;* two chapters in *The Calligrapher's Handbook*, ed. H. Child; 'Costing Work'. *The Scribe*, Winter 1988. Book in progress: *Formal Scripts*, co-authored with Stan Knight.

Recent exhibitions: SSI exhibitions 1951-89; ITC Center, New York; Alden Biesen, Belgium; Devon Guild of Craftsmen; recent Letter Exchange exhibitions.

Shakespeare Quotation

'Blow winds . . .' was done for submission to the recent Society of Scribes and Illuminators Shakespeare exhibition. It was, however, done after another piece, 'I know a bank . . .' (**1**) and is by way of a contrast in mood. I had taken the latter text for a series of about twenty examples of variations in

1. Extract from *A Midsummer Night's Dream*. This formed the starting point of 'Blow winds . . .' in that I wanted to choose another Shakespeare quotation capable of a very different visual interpretation.

29

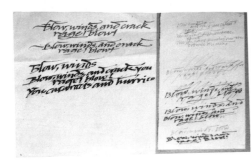

2. First ideas in a sketch book of possible styles for the writing.

3. First pencil rough of the shape produced by the whole speech.

spacing for a lecture on the use of space in calligraphy. The piece illustrated here is the culmination of that body of work. Naturally enough, in view of the words, it finally had a rather 'sweet' flavour. I now wanted to do something more intense and dramatic – so the quotation from *King Lear* was chosen.

First thoughts were about how the texture of the writing might suit the words, shown here in my quick notes (**2**). The first pencil rough of the whole speech (**3**) seemed too large an amount of text to deal with in the time available to me, and, as I had a feeling that the background was going to play as important a part as the text, I decided to concentrate on a shorter passage of text. I developed my ideas further in a sketchbook, including a suggestion for the background (**4**).

As 'I know a bank . . .' had been done in my gouache resist medium (gouache paint over which I paint waterproof ink) I was determined to do this one differently. The colour notes I made suggested that the text might be in watercolour on a coloured paper. (**5**) shows an attempt to put some positive colour in the writing, but this seemed very tame.

5. An initial attempt to bring colour into the background.

4. Further sketchbook ideas for letterforms and flourishes; early experiments for the background.

My next attempt (**6**) was done in gouache resist, which allowed me to introduce more colour in the background. At these stages I was concentrating on the colour and brushmarks used in the background and had for the moment put aside thoughts about the texture of the writing.

6. I then used gouache resist to introduce more colour.

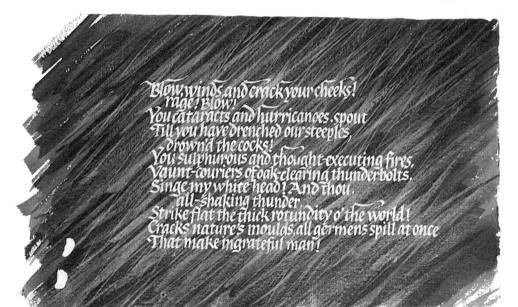

At the next stage (**7**) I tried to bring the writing and background to some conclusion, using watercolour and inks in the background. I also worked towards giving some movement and drama to the text by means of scale, position and diagonal inclination; here the texture of the writing was closer to that of the original roughs.

7. Experimenting with watercolour and ink for the background.

This attempt gave rise to two problems: the paper, although a suitable colour, proved to be an unstable surface under the application of so much ink,

and putting a strong black over such a dark background led to some illegibility. A second version on a slightly different paper was better but the ink bled unhappily from the bamboo pen here and there, and the background was still lighter than I wanted. I now started to think of making the piece's intended mounts play an integral part in the scheme of things. I produced a mount where I extended the painting of the background and included a thin white inlay (**8**).

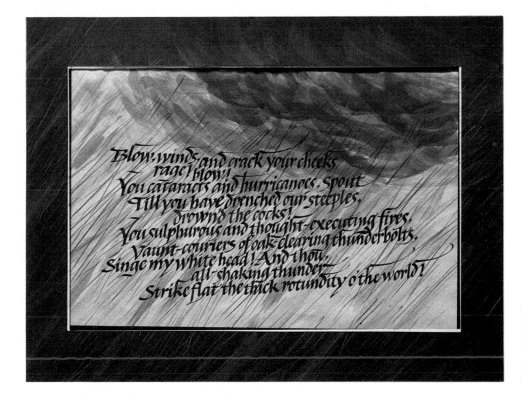

8. A rough including a painted mount.

The finished piece. (Right) Exhibition piece, 'Blow winds . . .' 526 × 374 mm (20 × 14½ in) Gouache resist with inks and watercolour on a cream laid hand-made paper.

As I was still not happy with the overall result, I decided, after all, to revert to the resist medium. A tougher paper, slightly warmer in colour, was chosen, and the next attempt seemed more successful. Two applications of the background inks were used to give subtle variations to the 'rain' textures and a final overlay of watercolour was added to the background when the inks had dried. I retained the idea of the painted mount. I did some colour trials on paper and card (**9**), realizing that slightly different shades would be needed to achieve a similar result on both materials.

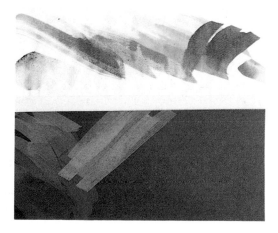

9. Experimenting on paper and card to see how the colours react to the various materials.

Time had now run out, and although I felt fairly pleased with this piece the writing did not have quite the vigorous rhythm I had in mind – one day I may try another version.

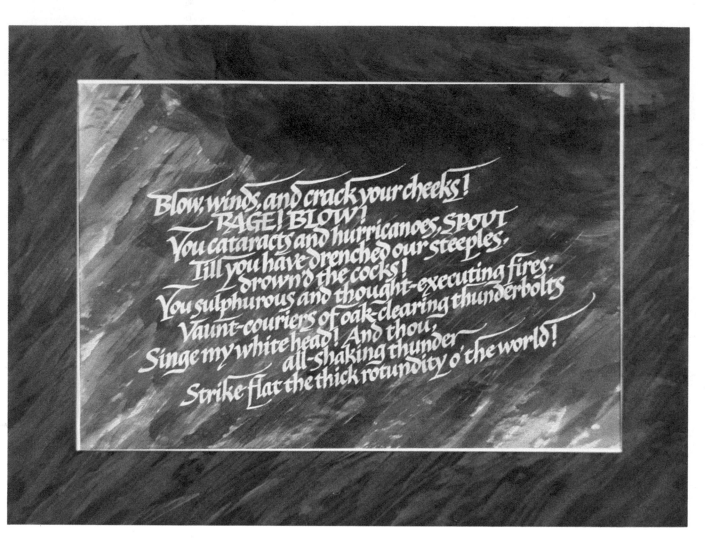

Christmas Card

I set out to achieve several ends in the design of this Christmas card. First, I had decided to do a small piece, which would remain half-finished, as a teaching aid to show the process of engraving letters on wood. At much the same time I was thinking of a short line of text which might form the basis for discussion at a workshop on greetings cards – something which would act as a focus for consideration of ways in which letterforms and their arrangements can suggest the meaning and sound of words. It seemed sensible to incorporate these two requirements in one piece. I also wanted to use this piece to develop my thoughts on the pointed italic letter – something I had always felt a bit awkward about, but now had to reconsider for a book of scripts on which I was working. Fortunately, a pointed italic seemed to fit the words I had in mind for the Christmas card. I had also been invited to produce something for this book and it seemed that a wood engraving might add to its

variety; this meant that the engraving would have to be completed, whereas I had intended to leave it incomplete, but that seemed a minor consideration as records were being kept of each stage of the making process.

The roughs show the development of the lettering, and the detailing involved. The meaning and sound of the words was continuously in mind. I used lemonwood – intentionally, as I had no previous experience of it and it might be used by the students in a forthcoming workshop. The wood had been bought before this piece of work was formulated, and its size and shape (140 × 36 mm/5½ × 1⅜ in) had a little effect (but appropriately, I think) on the layout and the degree to which the letters are condensed. Finally, the central word was used in outline to allow for the inclusion of further colours, maybe to be applied by hand. In a general sort of way I took into account that the final edition would be hand printed, possibly by the simple process of burnishing the wood through the paper.

1. First rough idea written with a fiber-tipped pen.

2. Some of the rough drawings of details of shapes and flourishes.

3. Rough drawing of the word sequence for the card.

4. A more detailed rough in which I began to experiment with colour within the central word.

5. A final detailed rough written with fiber-tipped pens.

6. Tracing of the drawing ready to be transferred to the block. The image must of course appear in reverse on the block to print the right way round.

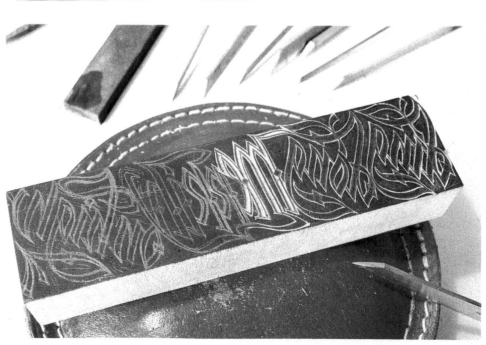

7. Engraving part-complete, showing the block in position on the sandbag and the tool used for outlining the letters.

The finished piece.
Wood engraved Christmas card
140 × 37 mm (5½ × 1½ in)
Printed in black on Japanese
paper, ready to be mounted on
coloured card. This is a final
proof.

WERNER SCHNEIDER

Studio: Am Langen Land 2, D-5928 Bad Laasphe, West Germany, tel: 01049-2754 453

Born in West Germany in 1935

Member of Society of Scribes, New York since 1982; the Type Directors Club, New York since 1985

Calligraphic training: Werkkunstschule, Wiesbaden (1954-58) under Professor Friedrich Poppl. Currently Professor of Graphic Design at the Fachhochschule, Wiesbaden

Recent commissions: Exclusive type design for H. Berthold AG Berlin (Munich); book design for publishing houses

Main publication: *Schrift: Analyse-Layout-Design*, in preparation; reproductions of Werner Schneider's work have appeared in many international publications

Recent exhibitions: Has exhibited widely in Europe, USA, Israel, Japan and India

---

Text by William Morris

See finished piece on page 38.

This work was done on the occasion of the 150th anniversary of the birth of William Morris and was commissioned by the Humanities Research Center of the University of Texas. (*See* finished piece on page 38.) A major calligraphic exhibition, containing some 150 pieces, was opened on 24 March 1984 to commemorate the great innovator of the Arts and Crafts Movement, especially for his contribution to the art of the book and of lettering.

The university's brief was to select significant quotations by William Morris and to interpret them calligraphically. The choice of calligraphy as the medium had its roots in Morris's philosophy. In his own work, Morris went back to the true source of occidental letterform, especially the classical Roman letters that were rediscovered in the Renaissance. This is what I used as the basis of my work on the original English version of the text. The German translation text was written in square Roman capitals. Both text passages were written with a metal pen, using watercolour. The illuminated letter as well as the palm leaf were inlayed with pure gold leaf. The background to the letter is watercolour. The work, which is in the possession of the University of Texas, was done on hand-made paper.

Quotation by Albert Einstein

This work was done on the occasion of the recent international exhibition on the art of the book in Leipzig. The theme of the exhibition was to be an artistic debate about the fear of war. (*See* finished piece on page 41.)

I chose this quotation by Albert Einstein, not only for its content but also because it offered interesting visual possibilities. I endeavoured to convey the strong meaning of the heading and its urgency in an appropriate manner while creating an arresting image. The visual concept for the heading – appeal to the peoples of the world – was the starting point of the piece and the main text served almost as a textural background to it.

The heading was written with a Japanese brush, the spontaneity of the strokes and the choice of red as a colour seeming appropriate to the words,

THE WORK that is to be its
WENN EIN WERK DIE ZUFRIEDENHEIT
creator's delight, must demand
DES SCHŒPFERS WIDERSPIEGELN SOLL,
all the resources of one's being –
SO MUSS ES DEN ANFORDERUNGEN VON HAND
hands, heart and head. Only in such
HERZ UND GEIST ENTSPRECHEN. NUR SO LOHNT
wise is labour worthy, and only after
SICH DIE MUHE UND NUR SO WIRD DIE BEDINGUNG
such fasion may the craftsman become
ERFULLT, IN DER SICH DER HANDWERKER ZUM
an artist also. *Soll das Werk den Meister*
KUNSTLER WANDELT – SOLL DAS WERK DEN MEISTER
loben. Surely the spirit which gives mean-
LOBEN – NATURLICH IST DER GEIST, DER SCHILLERS WORTE
ing to Schiller's words, must be the same
BELEBT, DER GLEICHE, DEN AUCH HERR MORRIS FUHLT.
spirit which Mr. Morris feels, and feeling
DENN SOLCHER GEIST KANN NUR ERFUHLT WERDEN,
it, reveals his worth and finds his joy
UM DESSEN FREUDE UND WEISHEIT GETREU ZU ERKENNEN.
in being ever faithful to its wisdom.

The finished piece (Left).
Text by William Morris (1984)
620 × 500 mm (24 × 19½ in)
Hand-made paper with deckle
edge; metal pens, watercolour and
gold leaf.

although I experimented with various colours for the background (**1** *and* **2**),
I tried out various versions of this heading until I found the one that worked
best with the text of the actual quotation. The text was first written out
roughly on tracing paper to work out the arrangement of the words and
lengths of lines. I chose a Roman inscriptional form and integrated the text of
the quotation over the heading.

This piece is in the possession of the German Library Museum in Leipzig.

This is the quotation by Albert Einstein which I chose for my piece:

APPEAL TO THE PEOPLES OF THE WORLD
'Behind secret walls the means of our mass extermination are being perfected

1. Rough of the heading on grey
Roma hand-made paper.

2. Experimenting with a different background.

with feverish haste. If this goal is achieved, the contamination of the air space and with it the destruction of all life on earth, would enter the realm of technical possibilities and everything seems to lead to this disastrous course. Every step appears like the inevitable consequence of the preceding one. On the horizon the spectre of wholesale destruction looms ever more clearly. We can only go on warning and warning again. We cannot wane in our efforts to tell the peoples of the world, and especially their governments, of the unheard-of catastrophe which they are conjuring up with all certainty if they do not radically alter their attitude to each other and their understanding of the future. Our world is being threatened by a crisis the extent of which appears to escape those who hold the power to reach important decisions to the good or to the bad. The unleashed force of the atom has changed

everything – except our thought processes. In this way we glide towards a disaster beyond comparison. If human life is to be preserved, we need to evolve a fundamentally different way of thinking. To avert the threat of destruction has become one of the most pressing issues of our time.'

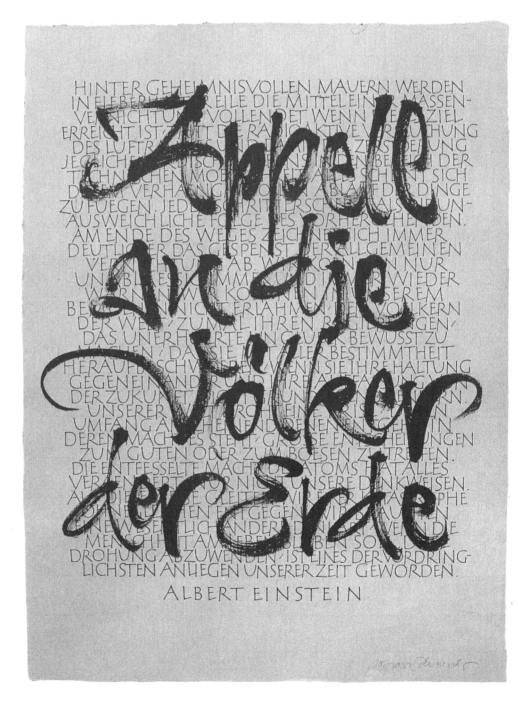

The finished piece.
Quotation by Albert Einstein
670 × 480 mm (26 × 19 in)
Watercolour on hand-made paper.

Commemorative Piece – William Morris

This work was also done on the occasion of the William Morris jubilee at the University of Texas. I personally regard this piece as one of my favourites, both from the point of view of content as well as of visual appeal. (*See* finished piece on page 44.)

1. Initial rough with a landscape format. The colours are dull green to black on white paper.

The large capitals are based on the timeless beauty of the monumental Roman capitals, supreme in the western tradition. These historical letterforms never cease to fill me with admiration. Here these letters were written spontaneously with a wooden stick and watercolour on handmade paper. A few drafts were made, trying out a variety of compositions and experimenting with various colours (see **1** *and* **2**). The sturdy wooden stick when used with watercolours allows for a nuanced painted result on the rough surface of the hand-made paper. The actual quotation was written in italic with a metal pen.

In this piece I strove for a visualization appropriate to the quote. This text has a special meaning for me as a type designer. In this technical age, the engineer has conquered letterforms through the development of electronic typesetting systems and debased them to pure technical concepts. This quotation, pointing to the artistic dimension of letter creation, if timely in Morris's day, has acquired a singular urgency in ours.

The finished piece. (*See* page 44)
Commemorative piece – William Morris
620 × 500 mm (24 × 19½ in)
Hand-made paper, wooden stick, metal pen, watercolour.

WILLIAM MORRIS:
The letters should
be designed
by an artist,
and not
en engineer.

2. The upright composition which
preceded the final piece.

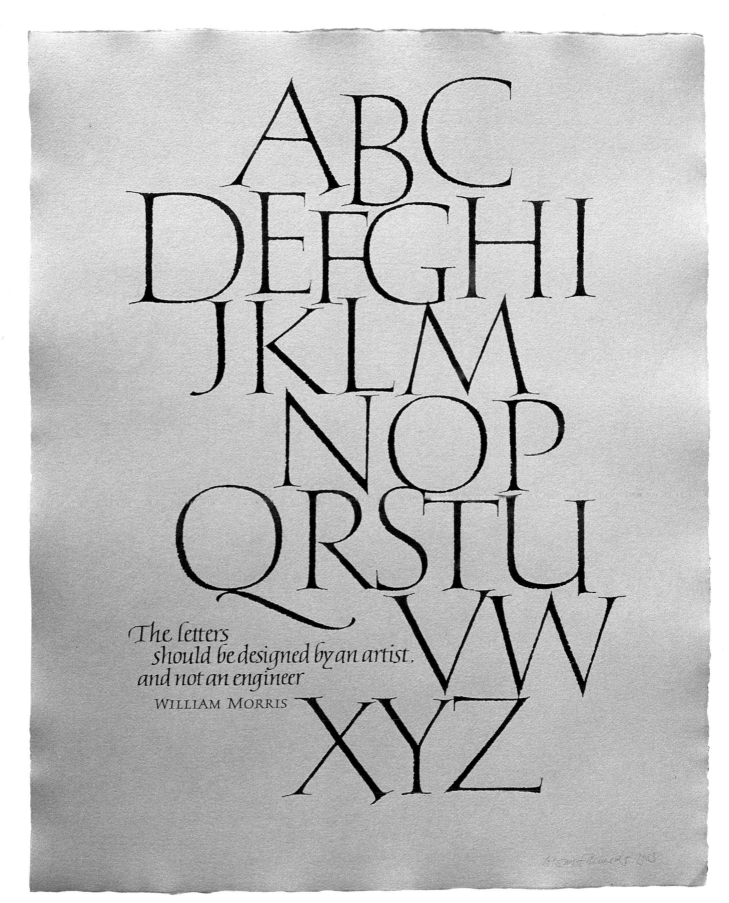

ABC
DEFGHI
JKLM
NOP
QRSTU
VW
XYZ

The letters
should be designed by an artist.
and not an engineer
WILLIAM MORRIS

44

ETHNA GALLACHER

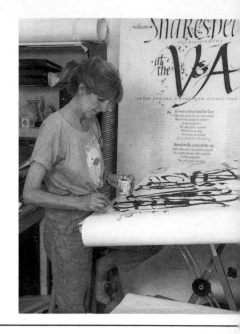

Studio: 9 Jamieson Avenue, Fairlight, Sydney, N.S.W. 2094, Australia
Born in England in 1940
Fellow of the Society of Scribes and Illuminators since 1988; member of the Australian Society
of Calligraphers

Calligraphic training: Glasgow School of Arts under Olivia Roberts; Digby Stuart College,
Roehampton Institute (1986-87) under Ann Camp, Gaynor Goffe, Tom Perkins and Jen
Lindsay

Recent commissions: Victoria & Albert Museum; Wolthard Friedrich

Main publications: Reproductions of Ethna Gallacher's work have appeared in *Calligraphy in
Australia*, Peter Taylor; *Mastering Calligraphy*, Tom Gourdie

Recent exhibitions: SSI exhibition; Paperpoint, London

Shakespeare Scroll

In spring of 1988 I was approached by the V & A Enterprises of the Victoria
and Albert Museum to be their 'resident calligrapher' as part of their Easter
holiday promotion.

For a two-week period and for four hours each day, my main brief was to
inscribe gift vouchers in the V & A shop. I was also to demonstrate, to talk
about my work and show how a modern-day scribe exists in the age of the
printed word. I could also give advice about classes and materials.

I decided that while I was there, I would work on a large piece on which I

The finished piece.
Shakespeare banner for Victoria &
Albert Museum (detail of centre
piece).
Large scroll, several feet high.
Ink on paper.

could build each day. This would give me an opportunity to talk about design, layout, texture, scale, and materials in the framework of a finished piece rather than isolated demonstration fragments. The large scroll, part of which can be seen hanging behind me on page 45, is the result.

I chose William Shakespeare for the universality of the quotations and the availability of the texts. Before I took up residence, I designed the core element of the scroll, planning to build the rest of the quotations around this. Once established in the shop, where I was positioned at a desk, I selected a quote each day, did a minimum of pre-planning and went ahead.

It proved to be a valuable and interesting vehicle which gave me a purpose for being there. I wanted to attract attention to the calligraphy so it had to be large. I hoped visitors to the shop would see it from some distance and feel interested enough to take a closer look. I think it worked. Several people came back a few days later to see the progress of the scroll.

There is a large range of sizes of lettering in this piece from the 38 mm (1½ inch) pen to a 0.3 mm wide nib and so it creates a vast range of textures. The 'core element' developed into a sort of logo and from it I developed smaller scrolls and fragments of the main piece. I had many lengthy and interesting conversations with customers and visitors to the museum. I talked my head off about what I like to do best and consequently had a wonderful time. It remains the highlight of my calligraphic year.

Scheherazade Panel

This piece was an attempt to recreate the spirit of *The Arabian Nights* – stories that always held a great fascination for me. The word Scheherazade, which was the name of the Sultana, had a great visual as well as aural appeal and it seemed to me to be a logical 'peg' from which the rest of the work could spring. Roman capitals were not my initial choice, as I had envisaged a more expressive, spontaneous style. But after trial and error, Roman capitals seemed to hang together well and the length of the word called for a horizontal shape. Also, starting off with this strong, fairly conservative letter form gave me opportunities to exploit the rest of the text with flourishes and abstract symbols. These decorative elements served as a backdrop to the word itself and suggested the use of sparkling colours, reminiscent of oriental courts.

The finished piece.
Scheherazade panel
375 × 920 mm (14¾ × 36 in)
Gouache, bronze powder, gum
arabic on blue-black paper.

The subject demanded a dark background – the night sky. The paper I chose is not quite black, more a very dark blue. I knew gold was essential though probably not in solid form. Mixing gouache with bronze powder and a drop or two of gum arabic gave me the sort of shimmering gold effect I was after. For the rest of the text I chose bright exciting colours like purples,

Detail of the finished piece reproduced actual size.

48

pinks, and turquoises and really the piece grew after that. I was lucky! All the lettering was of course western, but to emphasize the Arabian feel I looked at Arabic script and attempted to evoke its characteristics with the flourishes I used in the background.

The music of Rimsky-Korsakov was a great influence. I hoped to capture in visual terms the mood and excitement of his Suite for Orchestra – *Scheherazade*. I had intended to write some sort of text as an explanation of the piece, but later I decided to abandon it concentrating more or less solely on the 'atmosphere' of the piece.

Detail of early ink sketch – the lettering here is also shown to the actual size.

Calligraphic Wall Hanging

I have always been attracted by large scale lettering since I saw my father sharpen a piece of balsa wood to a chisel edge so that he could obtain larger letters than his available range of pen sizes would permit. Later as a teacher, I enjoyed moving my whole arm around over a blackboard, using the side of the chalk to make larger-than-life letters. On a visit to the British Museum in 1988 the Keeper of Oriental MSS showed a group of us a huge scroll with a very dramatic black image on it. It was the symbol of a tiger.

All these influences and memories are tied up in this piece, I suppose. As a follow-up to the visit to the British Museum I started to experiment with the largest pen I could find – a 38 mm (1½ inch) pen. Using this size of pen and black ink on white paper can produce very exciting and powerful results. I moved through different ideas for colours and eventually focused on using a palette of three colours of ink plus water, blending the colours as I worked. I did one stroke with one colour of ink, then refilled the pen with another colour and finished the letter while the first stroke was still wet, allowing the colours to merge. The results were interesting and sometimes unpredictable,

49

EXTRACTS FROM
TWENTY
SIX
LETTERS

AND JOURNALS OF
KATHERINE MANSFIELD

The finished piece.
Wall-hanging – 'Twenty-six letters'.
Coit pen and coloured inks on cream Heritage paper.
In the possession of Christopher Jarman.

but with a little forethought I could see I might achieve exciting effects.

It is natural for a calligrapher to experiment with the alphabet – it is the tool of our trade. I tend to favour the upright format and that was how the twenty-six letters evolved but, as I worked through these colour blendings, I started to superimpose letters on top of one another. This can be difficult if the text is to be read and be recognizable but the shape of the alphabet is such a familiar image that in this case at least, it posed few problems.

As I worked on the alphabet, I became conscious of the negative shapes which were created, so I developed the idea of the twenty-six letters further – within and without these negative shapes, I wrote out twenty-six extracts from the letters and journals of Katherine Mansfield. These quotations are in a much smaller size – not too small as to get lost beside the large alphabet – yet not too big as to compete and therefore cancel the impact of the larger image. The placing of the title, *Twenty-Six Letters*, and its size were crucial decisions too, but I was helped by a convenient flourish which swept out to the right and seemed to want to cradle the title.

The work was done on a very large sheet of cream Heritage paper. It took the large writing very well but I had some difficulty with the small text.

EWAN CLAYTON

Author's photograph by Jeanne Masoero

Studio: 70 Keymer Road, Hassocks, W. Sussex BN6 8OP, Tel: 07918 3747
Born in England in 1956
Member of Letter Exchange since 1988, the Guild of St Joseph & St Dominic, Ditchling since 1983

Calligraphic Training: Digby Stuart College, Roehampton Institute (1979-80) under Ann Camp. Awarded 1st Craft Fellowship in calligraphy to be offered by Crafts Council, 1981. Has taught widely in the United Kingdom and North America and is currently a Visiting Lecturer at Digby Stuart College. He also works as a consultant to the Document Research Programme in the System Sciences Laboratory at Zerox P.A.R.C. California

Recent commissions: London, Chicago, Minneapolis, Reykjavic

Main publications: Ewan Clayton's work is reproduced in *Contemporary British Lettering* by Michael Taylor and in Heather Child's *Calligraphy Today II*. He has written many articles and book reviews for *Crafts* magazine; *Benchmark; Calligraphy Review*; and the journals of the Society of Scribes and Illuminators and Letter Exchange

Recent exhibitions: Many exhibitions at home and abroad since 1980

Banner for Worth Abbey

The first of the three pieces of work whose design process I want to share with you is a banner. Here the design was largely controlled by decisions that others had already taken and by very clear ideas of how, where and when it would be used. It was one of a set made for the Benedictine Monastery at Worth in Sussex, where I was a monk for some years. The large modern church demanded clear, bold forms. The banners were intended for the pre-Easter festival commemorating Christ's joyful entry into Jerusalem. The red cloth matched the colour of the vestments the monks would wear. The banner was made to hang between two others with interlaced palm designs upon them. To balance with these, I chose one word and wrote it in a flourished italic form reflecting the curves of the palms. In fact, my initial sketch was made on transparent paper laid on top of the palm design so that I knew I was echoing its character.

The final piece used a lightweight cloth in a cotton and polyester mix. The letters were cut out of stiff white paper and stuck down with a rubber cement glue. I made the patterns for these cut letters with double-pencils; that is to say, a pencil fixed to either side of a piece of wide planking long enough for me to write standing up with the paper on the floor. Some of the letters are several feet high. Cheap materials have been used deliberately, so the banner has a life of only a couple of years and must then be renewed.

This account of the design appears straightforward, if not prosaic. However the unwritten assumption behind such an account of my work is that a direct and responsive way of working has only become possible for me because I have spent considerable time and effort in a more formal analysis of our western traditions of lettermaking. It *should* be obvious as to students of dance, music, painting and sculpture that a period of formal study is useful, but surprisingly this is not widely appreciated. Perhaps because lettering has been subject to a process of mechanisation for over 500 years, people's

perceptions of letterform appear to have been shaped by this mechanical perspective. As long as they retain a basically passive attitude towards letter shapes instead of seeing them as offering possibilities for intelligent and genuinely creative work, lettermaking will be denied the public recognition it deserves. Having stressed the root importance of a sound grasp of the tradition let us consider several pieces of work that touch on that vital aspect of 'mastering' the tradition – the movement of this knowledge down from the head to the heart. Only in this way is the tradition made a living one.

The finished piece.
Palm Sunday banner for Worth
Abbey
3.4 × 1.1 m (11 × 3½ ft)
Cloth and paper.

Calligraphic Study

This piece of work, a study entitled 'There are Palaces Everywhere', differs from the first in having had very few external constraints on its design, so that the words themselves played an intrinsic part in the search for a form. The calligrapher Irene Wellington once said that the hardest thing to write was 'stark truth'; the difficulties I encountered with this design helped me to understand her better.

I had begun to experiment with building letters up from dots, a method I had developed to circumvent the monastery printer's difficulty in printing significant areas of black without the paper remaining stuck to his roller! I discovered this technique had interesting potentials. It allowed me to shade letters, to handle weight in unsuspected ways and to make letters within one word which incorporated different perspectives and viewpoints (**1**). This approach was suggested by David Hockney's work. Later I began to experiment by combining colour with this technique but only in a flat two-dimensional way (**2**).

1. Lettering used on the cover of a pamphlet for St Peter's Monastery, Dulwich. Note the different viewpoints – one looks down on the final H, sideways into the R and up at the first H.

2. Detail from an incomplete work, 'Crucifixion, Compassion, Emptiness, Resurrection'. Gouache on Chatham vellum paper. The piece moves in colour to grey through green and blue ending in orange.

The up-shot of these experiments was that I thought of using the dots as a way of making this particular commission. I would make the dots glow from a dark background – tiny atoms of light that came together in the mind's eye to build 'palaces'. I was not at all happy with the result. It looked sugary and trite, with the hint of a fairground. In this form I just could not agree with the message the words seemed to carry (**3**).

I abandoned dots. I drew the letter forms in rough outline, massing them together for strength (**4**). Then I took this one step further, drawing the spaces

3. Work on Japanese paper in gouache underpainted in white.

between the letters as shapes in their own right. This gave a 'Belle Epoch' feel to the words. Again, I felt entirely opposed to the frivolity I seemed to be conveying (**5**). After six weeks of effort, on the point of resigning the commission as something for which I did not want to be responsible, I sat down, finally determined to overcome my resistance and explore the words fully. Why had I felt my work so far to be a travesty of truth? What truth? I discovered I did agree with the words, but only if they were not indicative of some irresponsible fantasy, but as spoken by the voice of one who had suffered, who had confronted the illusions that death reveals, and from such ruthless destruction emerged gentle, vastly free and radiant. 'My house burnt down. I own a better view of the rising moon,' wrote Basho, the celebrated Zen poet. From this realization, my final design sprang, expressive of Blake's words that 'joy and woe are woven fine'. This realization that 'there are palaces everywhere' comes through a painful exposure, and is an awe-ful statement of frightening self-forgetfulness (**6** *overleaf*).

4. First sketch for massed letterforms. I intended to flood a mixture of colour through these letter shapes.

5. Second sketch for massed letterforms. The spaces rather than the letterforms are drawn here. Subsequently I abandoned this idea, but its tangled undergrowth of forms is suggestive of the solution I finally adopted.

The finished piece.
Piece commissioned by Lorna Low
203 × 267 mm (8 × 10½ in)
Eighteenth-century Dutch paper;
written with a quill and black stick
ink mixed with stick vermillion,
and gilding in powder gold.

The letterforms were developed from doodles executed several months
earlier and now found useful. They take the calligrapher's understanding of
letters built from overlapping forms one stage further and overlap dissimilar
forms in different ways (*see* below). I took this technical experiment one step
further in another piece (top of opposite page). I show this here because on a
technical level it was a spin-off from the 'Palaces' piece.

An ordinary pen-made E (**1**) is
made from two overlapped forms
(**2**). Once the overlapped forms are
mentally distinguished (**3**), they can
be varied independently of each
other (**4**). The independently
varied forms can be reunited as
new outlines (**5**).

(1)

(2)

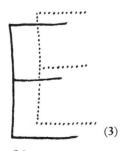

(3)

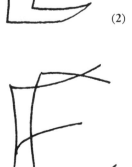

(4)

(5)

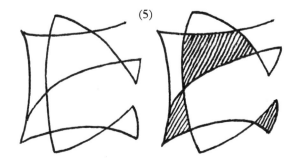

'Space becoming significant',
190 × 286 mm (7½ × 11¼ in).
Written with a quill; black stick
ink mixed with vermillion on
eighteenth-century Dutch paper.
This piece results from reading
Henry Moore on his two and three
piece sculptures. He talks of them
as experiments in eliminating
something in order to discover
what is essential – space then
becomes significant.

Design for a Logo

The final piece I want to show you is different again. It is a design for a logo,
a simple piece of direct penwork. The logo was for a week's retreat at
Glastonbury Abbey, held one thousand years after the death of its famous
abbot St Dunstan. Several levels of association crystallized with very little
preparatory work into the finished form; what work I had to do was in
combining these associations in my imagination. This piece was the product of
a meditation. St Benedict says in his Rule 'Let us prefer nothing whatsoever to
Christ' so at the heart of the logo are two Christological symbols. Firstly, the
Pascal candle used at the Easter night service as the symbol of Resurrection, of
the 'light' of Christ, freeing and guiding, just like the pillar of fire for the
Israelites in the desert. The second symbol is of Christ Sun of Justice – the
overwhelming symbol of the Kingdom of Heaven, Christ's vision of God, that
to which he leads. The sun also has particular Benedictine associations, for at
the end of his life Benedict had a vision of the world taken up in a sun-beam,
as by God, sustaining and giving life to all. This was a vision of the goodness
of creation and its complete inter-penetration by God, and it characterizes
Benedict's rule of life for monks.

  A further layer of imagery was provided by a story told about Dunstan. His
mother Cynethryth was in church shortly before her child was born when all
the candles were blown out save the one she held. From that, all the people
rekindled their lights. A holy man said that the child she bore should give
light to all England by his holy living. So another interpretation of this design

1. Early sketches for the logo. The finished design, however, was arrived at with very little preparation.

is of Cynethryth's taper, or Dunstan's light, surrounded by many smaller lights making one body.

Additionally, the circle stands for the Benedictine idea of balance: the circle is the unassertive product of perfectly balanced vertical and horizontal elements. There is the polarity of day (sun) and night (candle). There is the image of fire as a symbol of prayer, and here I remember the burning bush of Moses. The sun design optically moves, which gives us the 'cosmic dance'. The letters I subsequently employed derive from a manuscript written in England around the time of Dunstan's death. They have an underlying circular form (slightly compressed here for stability) to give a relationship between the letters and the shape of the logo itself.

So, there we have it. Three works all bringing out different aspects of the design process, attention to environment, attention to words and attention to our own creative patterns of thought. The theme I have picked up here and which I hope to encourage in my work, is an ever-increasing ability to listen, to think and work with a contemplative attitude. I want to assert the value of creating out of ways of *being* rather than out of ways of *doing*. I think this is what Irene Wellington referred to when she talked about the difficulty of writing 'stark truth'.

The finished piece.
Logo design for Glastonbury Abbey
89×102 mm ($3\frac{1}{2} \times 4$ in).

BRODY NEUENSCHWANDER

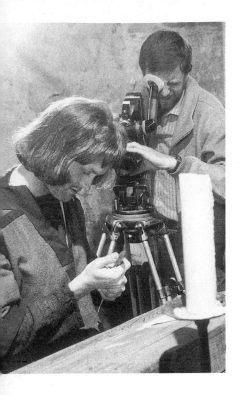

Author's photograph by courtesy of the BBC

Studio: 13 Heath Drive, Hampstead, London NW3, tel: 01-431 4143
Born in USA in 1958
Fellow of the Society of Scribes and Illuminators since 1985; member of Letter Exchange since 1988

Calligraphic training: Roehampton Institute (1983-85) under Ann Camp, Tom Perkins, Gaynor Goffe. Assistant to Donald Jackson (1987-88). Presently teaching at Digby Stuart College, Roehampton Institute

Recent commissions: the Embassy of the United States in London; the British Broadcasting Corporation; the Society of Scribes and Illuminators; the Egypt Exploration Society; Westminster Cathedral; English Heritage; Princeton University; The Lord Mayor of Westminster; the College of Arms; The Royal Academy of Dramatic Art

Main publications: *Order, Variety and Measure: the Creation of the Medieval Manuscript* (exhibition Catalogue) Princeton University; Some Thoughts on the Anglo-Saxon Exhibition at the British Museum, *The Scribe* (Journal of the SSI). Most recent reproductions of Brody Neuenschwander's work have appeared in: *Calligraphy Today*; *Contemporary Calligraphy* (Modern Scribes . . .); *The Calligrapher's Project Book*, Susanne Haines; *The Scribe*; *Calligraphy Review*.

Recent exhibitions: Museum of Fine Arts, Houston; Princeton University Library; Ruskin Gallery in Sheffield City Art Gallery; Warwick University Art Gallery; Paperpoint, London

Presentation Panel

John Donne's poem 'To Mr Tilman After He Had Taken Orders' was copied out in 1989 for Father T. E. Phipps to give to a friend at his ordination to the priesthood. The brief was to produce a framed panel, not overly large, that would present Donne's text in a way suitable to the grand occasion.

The length of the poem – fifty-four long lines – created problems in meeting this brief. Our expectations of framed panels arise largely from a response to paintings, which achieve a strong impact through the use of areas of colour. Short texts can achieve similar impact by being written boldly or in strong colours; but a lengthy written text whatever the colour or style, can easily fade into an overall featureless texture. It was therefore decided to write the poem out over areas of colour, an approach that was also used for the piece entitled 'Immanuel', which is reproduced on page 65. At this point a sliver of a design produced two years earlier surfaced to provide the basic idea of dark letters written on a shimmering gold ground, an arrangement that seemed to suit both the words and the occasion (**1**). A compact Gothic hand was chosen to

1. The fragment which provided me with a starting point for the poem.

LIGHT hEAD flIGHT SPREAD DREAMS LIKE GOSSAM

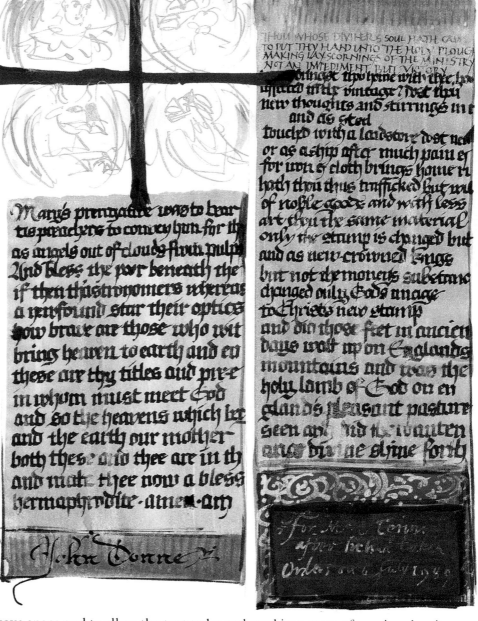

2. The first working rough.

save space and to allow the text to be gathered into areas of varying density. The letters appeared almost as individual brushstrokes used to pattern the surface of the gold.

It could be argued that this approach reduces legibility. In this case the text was well known to both giver and receiver and was being presented to commemorate an occasion, not to pass on information. It therefore seemed acceptable to compromise legibility somewhat for the sake of a stronger, more painterly impact. This is not to imply that the sense of the words is disregarded. On the contrary, the free and playful movement of the words over and beyond the columns of gold leaf is intended to heighten the transcendent themes of the poem.

A small rough (2) was first produced, using bronze powder mixed with gum arabic. Areas of colour were added to provide for the author's name and the dedication, and to serve as background to patterns in gold, which are of interest to me owing to my work as a textile designer. A large black cross was first used to head the left-hand column, but this rather funereal design was

Thou whose diviner soul hath caused thee now
    To put thy hand unto the holy plough,
Making lay-scornings of the ministry
    Not an impediment, but victory;
What bringst thou home with thee? how is
        thy mind
    Affected in the vintage? Dost thou find
New thoughts and stirrings in thee, and
            as steel
Touched with a loadstone, dost new motions
            feel?
    Or, as a ship after much pain and care,
    For iron and cloth brings home rich
            Indian ware?
Hast thou thus trafficked, but with far more
            gain
    Of noble goods, & with less time and pain?
Art thou the same materials as before,
    Only the stamp is changed, but no more?
And as new crowned kings alter the face,
But not the money's substance so hath grace,
Changed only God's old image by creation,
To Christ's new stamp, at this thy
            coronation?
    Or, as we paint angels with wings, because
    They bear God's message and
            proclaim his laws,
Since thou must do the like, & so must move,
Art thou new-feathered with celestial love?
    Dear, tell me where thy purchase lies,
            and show
    What thy advantage is above, below.
    But if thy gaining do surmount
            expression,
        Why doth the foolish world scorn
            that profession

Whose joys pass speech? Why do they
        think unmeet
That gentry should join families with it?
As if their day were only to be spent
In dressing, mistressing and compliment.
Alas poor joys, but poorer men, whose trust
    Seems richly placed in refined dust;
    For such are clothes and beauty, which
            though gay,
    Are at the best, but as sublimed clay.
Let then the world thy calling disrespect,
But go thou on, and pity their neglect.
What function is so noble, as to be
    Ambassador to God and destiny?
To open life, to give kingdoms to more
    Than kings give dignities; to keep
            heaven's door?
Mary's prerogative was to bear Christ, so
'Tis preachers' to convey him, for they, to
As angels out of clouds, from pulpits speak;
    And bless the poor beneath, the lame,
            the weak.
    If then th'astronomers, whereas
            they spy
A new-found star their optics magnify,
How brave are those who, with
            their engine can
Bring man to heaven and heaven again
            to man?
    These are thy titles and pre-eminences,
    In whom must meet God's grace,
            men's offices,
    And so the heavens which beget all
            things here,
And the earth our mother, which these
            things doth bear,
    Both these in thee are in thy calling
            knit,
    And make thee now a blessed
        hermaphrodite.

✝ John Donne ✝

To Mr O Connor after he had taken
    vows on Xxul july 1959

The finished piece. (Left) Commissioned presentation panel Gold leaf, gouache and gesso applied with quill and Chinese brush to Rives BFK paper.

replaced by a thinner cross surrounded by the evangelist symbols drawn quickly in gold. At this stage the two columns were cut apart and realigned to produce a more compact mass of gold.

A full-scale rough (not produced here, as it does not differ markedly from the final piece) was made, again using bronze powder rather than gold leaf. As always in the development of a piece, good ideas were jettisoned for the sake of the whole. At this size the areas of colour which had been acceptable in the previous rough drew the eye to the bottom of the page, and were therefore removed. This yielded a far more monumental composition consisting of two elements only: the cross and the columns of gold. The idea of patterning was retained below the right-hand column to balance the evangelist symbols upper left. On the rough this patterning was the result of many overpaintings as I felt my way forward. On the final panel the patterns consist of fleur-de-lis (a Marian symbol and therefore appropriate for a priest) in raised gold. Again the columns were cut apart and realigned, this time to produce a strong contrast and, when framed with narrow margins, rectangles of white which would serve as counterpoints to the rectangles of gold.

The lay-out was thus established, but it remained to devise a way of fixing the gold leaf which allowed it to be written on. The columns were marked out lightly in pencil on a sheet of Rives BFK paper, which was then soaked in water and stuck down wet to a smooth formica surface. The surface of the paper was then sized with thin rabbit glue and the sheets of gold leaf dropped onto the damp surface. When dry the gold was sized with rabbit glue to provide a good writing surface. The sheet was then allowed to dry completely and was lifted from the surface.

The gold was then dusted with sandarac powder and the text written with a quill and gouache. Afterwards the cross was quickly painted with a large Chinese brush. The evangelist symbols and fleur-de-lis were faintly sketched in with pencil and then drawn quickly with a quill and gesso, after which they were gilded. Fragments of gold leaf adhered directly to the paper owing to the rabbit glue, and these were allowed to remain. The piece was then framed in a dark metal frame equipped with thin strips of blackened wood to keep the glass off the gold.

The final effect of the piece is of a shimmering surface that changes with the light. In the brightest light the words are thrown into high relief and seem to hover above the surface in a way quite suitable to John Donne's words.

Panel with Hebrew Lettering

The words of the quotation occupied my mind for many months before I found a way of expressing their power in a calligraphic composition. In this text from the Book of Revelation the Apostle John restates the central lesson of the Old Testament – that God is with his people Israel – in the context of the New Testament revelation of Christ. Old Testament and New Testament are therefore intimately linked. It was my desire from the beginning to express this link by using the Hebrew word Immanuel (God with us) together with St John's text.

After several failed attempts I hit upon the idea of applying textured areas of bold colour to the paper using rollers and water-based lino ink. The writing would be done over these areas of colour, giving the impact that was essential to my concept of the piece. Large areas of yellow and orange were tried, with the texture running from one colour to the other. The division of the ground under the words seemed arbitrary and was abandoned, but the experiment

yielded areas of brilliant yellow with heavy black letters that had the strength and power for which I was searching. It was a simple matter to cut and reassemble these yellow and black fragments into strips, which made for sensible divisions of the text. The decision to divide these strips by bands of strong blue was spontaneous and cannot be explained, but it was on the strength of this combination that the large, abstract forms of the Hebrew letters, cut from black paper, could be added to the growing composition.

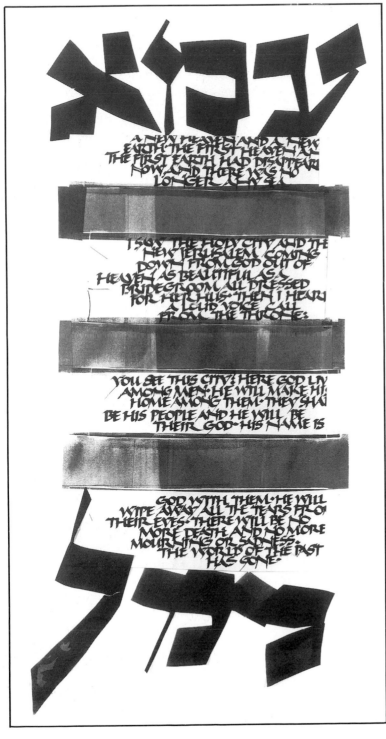

1. The bands of colour and the strips of text pasted in position.

The finished piece.
Panel with Hebrew lettering
190 × 126 mm (7½ × 5 in)
Water-based lino ink, Chinese
stick ink and cut paper letters on
Rives BFK paper.

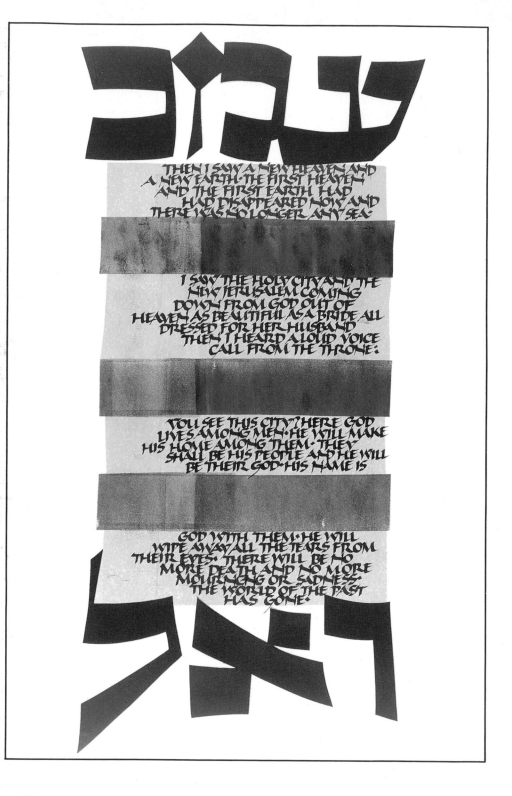

There were no significant changes to this basic idea, and only one rough was made (**1**). In the final piece the bands of colour and the arrangement of the text remained the same. The Hebrew letters were, of course, more carefully drawn and were pasted down quickly to avoid the need to press the piece while it was drying.

Shakespeare Poster

The design for this poster was commissioned by the Society of Scribes and Illuminators to advertise a travelling exhibition of modern calligraphy on the theme of Shakespeare. The brief was to provide a bold, highly calligraphic poster in two colours to be reproduced in A2, A3 and A4 (approximately 16½ × 23⅛, 11⅜ × 16½ and 8¼ × 11⅜ inches) sizes with changing venue information. Stationery and an invitation to a private view were also designed.

The exhibition had a secondary title, 'Dressing Old Words New', and so from the start it seemed appropriate to have modern calligraphy placed over a page from a Shakespeare first folio. The idea of a vastly enlarged reproduction of Shakespeare's signature followed quickly as a way of giving the poster an immediately recognizable identity.

The length of the words in the exhibition's title made it necessary to write it in condensed italics rather than capitals. Freely written italics would not have contrasted sufficiently with the enlarged signature and would have been less

1. The final paste-up prepared for the camera.

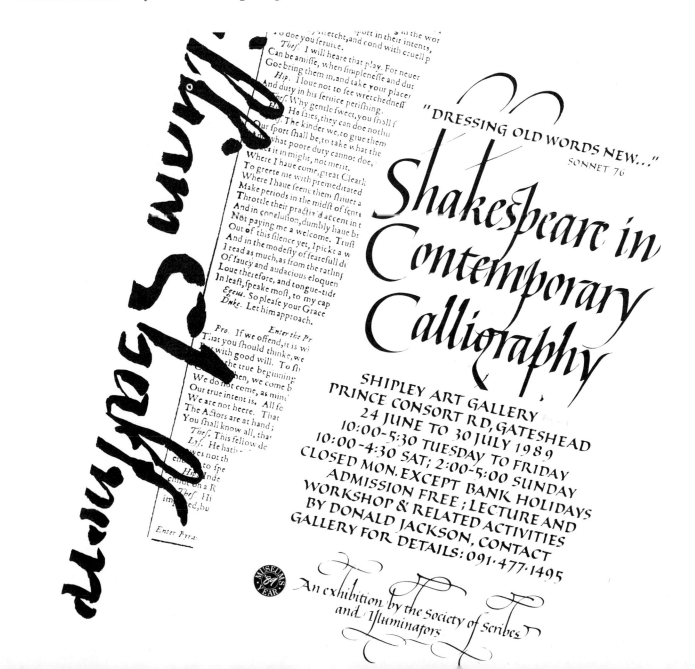

2. The rough guide I provided to the printer as a colour key.

The finished piece (overleaf). 276 × 193 mm (11 × 7½ in) Poster printed in two colours. In this book the poster was reproduced using a four-colour reproduction process. This is when the problems caused by the very fine hairlines in the calligraphy became apparent. The dots that make up the red colour cause the breaking up and filling of the finest white lines. When the poster was printed originally in two colours, this difficulty did not arise – the fine white lines being edged by a solid area of colour. This is an important point to remember when preparing calligraphic work for reproduction.

legible than the highly manipulated italics which were eventually chosen. These were produced by writing the words directly with a reed and then refining them afterwards with a pointed pen and brush. The title was reversed out photographically (**1**).

A large area below the title was reserved for the changing venue information, which was written with a quill using very legible but still calligraphic capitals. The italic heading is then echoed at the bottom of the poster by two heavily flourished lines of writing. The paste-up for this poster was complicated and a good deal was left to the printer, who was provided with a full-scale, full colour rough as a guide (**2**).

Phi. No, my noble Lord, it is not for you. I
It ouer, and it is nothing, nothing in the wor
Vnlesse you can finde sport in their intents,
Extreamely stretcht, and cond with cruell p
To doe you seruice.

Thes. I will heare that play. For neuer
Can be amisse, when simplenesse and dut
Goe bring them in, and take your places

Hip. I loue not to see wretchednesse
And duty in his seruice perishing.

Thes. Why gentle sweet, you shall s

Hip. He saies, they can doe nothir

Thes. The kinder we, to giue them
Our sport shall be, to take what the
And what poore duty cannot doe,
...es it in might, not merit.

Where I haue come, great Cleark
To greete me with premeditated
Where I haue seene them shiuer a
Make periods in the midst of sent
Throttle their practiz'd accent in
And in conclusion, dumbly haue br
Not paying me a welcome. Trust
Out of this silence yet, I pickt a w
And in the modesty of fearefull dt
I read as much, as from the rattlig
Of saucy and audacious eloquen
Loue therefore, and tongue-tide
In least, speake most, to my cap

Egeus. So please your Grace
Duke. Let him approach.

Enter the P

Pro. If we offend, it is w
That you should thinke, we
But with good will. To sh
...the true beginning
... then, we come b
We do not come, as mind
Our true intent is. All fo
We are not heere. That
The Actors are at hand;
You shall know all, that

Thes. This fellow do
Lys. He hath
...wes not th
enough to spe
Hip. Inde
...chue on a R
Thes. Hi
imp...ed, bu

Enter Pyra:

"DRESSING OLD WORDS NEW..."
SONNET 76

Shakespeare in Contemporary Calligraphy

WIGGINS TEAPE PAPERPOINT
130 LONG ACRE COVENT GDN·
LONDON WC2; 13 TO 23 MARCH 1989
MONDAY TO FRIDAY 9:15–4:45
9:15–1:00 ON 23 MARCH
CLOSED SATURDAY AND SUNDAY
ADMISSION FREE

An exhibition by the Society of Scribes and Illuminators

MARGARET DAUBNEY

Studio: 116 Westcombe Park Rd, London SE3 7RZ, Tel: 01-853 2717
Born in Nottingham, England in 1945
Fellow of the Society of Scribes and Illuminators since 1989

Calligraphic training: Studied with Ann Hechle before attending Digby Stuart College, Roehampton Institute (1984-88), tutored by Ann Camp, Gaynor Goffe, Tom Perkins and Gerald Fleuss. Teaches adult education classes and is a tutor on the Digby Stuart correspondence course.

Recent commissions: Alain Mazeran, Paris; Allied International Designers; Artists General Benevolent Institution; Barclays Bank Head Office; The Geological Society of London; Interflora International; London Borough of Tower Hamlets; The Royal Aeronautical Society; The Royal Yachting Association; Smith & Nephew plc; University of London, Goldsmith's College

Main publications: Reproductions of Margaret Daubney's work have appeared in *Florilège*, ed. Alain Mazeran

Recent exhibitions: SSI touring exhibition

Presentation Piece

In 1988 I was commissioned by Bernard Dunstan RA, Chairman of the Artists General Benevolent Institution, to write out a passage from the writings of St Makarios. The passage was a favourite of Donald Hamilton Fraser RA and was to be presented to him by the Council of the AGBI to mark his retirement as Chairman. It was a particularly interesting project because working to an artist introduces dimensions not encouraged when working for commercial clients, and also because I saw the project through to two quite different conclusions.

In his first letter, Bernard Dunstan wrote that he visualized the passage 'written in fairly traditional style'. The first draft of version **A** was an attempt to offer him something traditional without being too old-fashioned. Certain statements within the text can bear emphasis; these were used to create texture and were in capitals, with the rest of the text in lower case. I was aiming for a symmetrical lay-out, breaking lines at points where the sense dictated, but this was not working towards the end of the passage. I ruled up a lower guide line for this version, and the interlinear spacing needs correction.

WITHIN THE HEART ARE UNFATHOMABLE DEPTHS

There are reception rooms and

Detail of draft of **version A**.

WITHIN THE HEART
ARE UNFATHOMABLE DEPTHS

Version A: first draft

There are reception rooms and
bedchambers in it, doors and porches
and many offices and passages.
In it is the workshop of
righteousness and of wickedness.
In it is death · in it is life.

THE·HEART·IS·CHRIST'S·PALACE
THERE·CHRIST·THE·KING
·COMES·TO·TAKE·HIS·REST·
WITH·THE·ANGELS·AND·THE
·SPIRITS·OF·THE·SAINTS

and He dwelleth there walking within it
and placing His Kingdom there.
The heart is but a small vessel ;
and yet dragons and lions are there,
and there poisonous creatures
and all the treasures of wickedness ;
rough uneven paths are there
and gaping chasms.
There likewise is God, there are
the angels, there life and the
Kingdom, there light and
the apostles, the heavenly cities
and the treasures of grace.

ALL·THINGS·ARE·THERE

In version **B** I was trying a more personal approach. The text suggested the use of informal capitals rather than lower case and my aim was to create a block, rather than lines, of writing. This first draft was written spontaneously

WITHIN·THE·HEART
ARE UNFATHOMABLE DEPTHS
THERE ARE RECEPTION ROOMS
AND BEDCHAMBERS IN IT·
DOORS AND PORCHES·AND
MANY OFFICES AND PASSAGES·
IN IT IS THE WORKSHOP OF
RIGHTEOUSNESS AND OF
WICKEDNESS·IN IT IS DEATH·
IN·IT·IS·LIFE
THE HEART IS CHRIST'S
PALACE·THERE
CHRIST THE KING

Version B: detail of first draft

and freely – there were no guide lines, no initial doodles or roughs but I worked through the text aiming to create a rectangular shape and allowing the sense to dictate the letters. Much of this worked surprisingly well for a first rough, but probably the most important problem to be resolved was the unevenness of the texture. The lower part of the text block was too dense and needed some white spaces to balance with the top. Yet this was the rough chosen by the client mainly, I think, because he liked the shape.

I had to try to resolve the textural problems and to follow the sense of the text while keeping to the rectangular outline. In a later draft I selected some statements that appeared to me as specially important and wrote them larger and I discarded the straight left-hand edge in an attempt to let in more white space. I also experimented with colour.

Gradually the whole piece became more open and spacious. The contrast between large and small capitals was increased to make a more pleasing texture and more white space was introduced. The overall rectangular shape was preserved but the problem of the heavy-weight lower section had not been fully resolved. The passage was freely written. I ruled a line on which to write 'Within the heart' and then three further lines at 75mm (3 inch) intervals to use as markers so that I would not stray too far from the horizontal. The colour used throughout was dark blue watercolour, a little gold decoration, using transfer leaf on gum ammoniac, having been used as a highlight. The paper was hand-made Chatham Vellum. Overleaf you will find a reproduction of the piece I presented to the client.

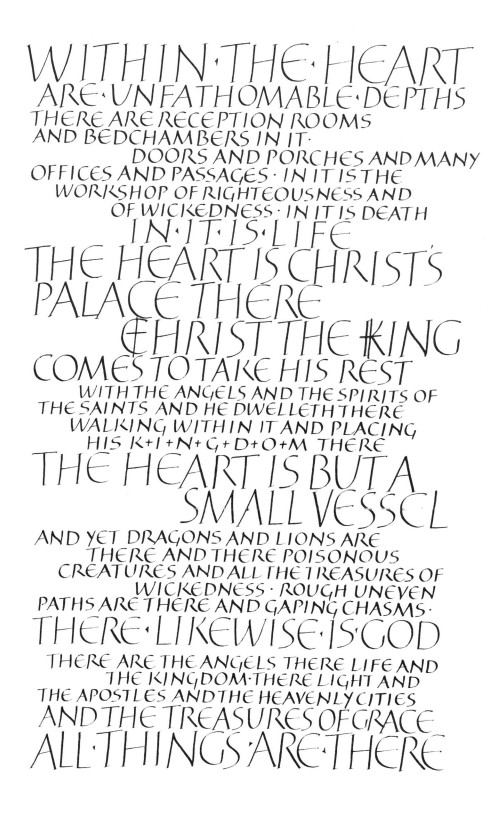

WITHIN·THE·HEART
ARE·UNFATHOMABLE·DEPTHS
THERE ARE RECEPTION ROOMS
AND BEDCHAMBERS IN IT·
DOORS AND PORCHES AND MANY
OFFICES AND PASSAGES· IN IT IS THE
WORKSHOP OF RIGHTEOUSNESS AND
OF WICKEDNESS· IN IT IS DEATH
IN·IT·IS·LIFE
THE HEART IS CHRIST'S
PALACE THERE
CHRIST THE KING
COMES TO TAKE HIS REST
WITH THE ANGELS AND THE SPIRITS OF
THE SAINTS AND HE DWELLETH THERE
WALKING WITHIN IT AND PLACING
HIS K+I+N+G+D+O+M THERE
THE HEART IS BUT A
SMALL VESSEL
AND YET DRAGONS AND LIONS ARE
THERE AND THERE POISONOUS
CREATURES AND ALL THE TREASURES OF
WICKEDNESS· ROUGH UNEVEN
PATHS ARE THERE AND GAPING CHASMS·
THERE·LIKEWISE·IS·GOD
THERE ARE THE ANGELS THERE LIFE AND
THE KINGDOM·THERE LIGHT AND
THE APOSTLES AND THE HEAVENLY CITIES
AND THE TREASURES OF GRACE
ALL·THINGS·ARE·THERE

Presented to
DONALD·HAMILTON·FRASER
by his friends on the Council of the AGBI in gratitude for his services as Chairman

1981 — 1987

The finished piece. (Left)
Presentation piece (Version B
chosen by client)
228 × 182 mm (9 × 7¼ in)
Hand-made Chatham Vellum
paper; watercolour; transfer gold
leaf on gum ammoniac.

Version **C** was an attempt to start with the words and to allow the design to grow out of them. This was a more complicated process, done purely for my own satisfaction, beginning with many sheets of doodles like the one below. I wanted to use capitals but wasn't sure what type of capitals, and the possibilities were endless. The idea of using touches of lower case grew out of writing the passage. The text is structurally unsophisticated, being a series of simple sentences strung together with 'ands'; I decided to use some of these conjunctions as decoration.

WITHIN
WITHIN
WITHIN THE
WITHIN

Version C: early doodles.

There are many similarities between versions B and C, but I think the finished version **C** (*overleaf*) works more successfully. Because there were no limitations on shape, I was able to break lines more successfully while still retaining the sense of the words, and to resolve the textural weaknesses. Whereas version B became lighter by becoming larger, this became lighter by becoming finer. The whole passage was written freely without any guide lines.

The text presents important ideas but the tone is not at all earnest and I felt that the use of informal capitals and the decorative spots of red echoed this. The colours are watercolour, the blue and green based on ultramarine. The vellum, which was a small, lightly marked skin, was stretched over board.

The finished piece. (Overleaf)
Version C
228 × 182 mm (9 × 7¼ in)
Vellum; watercolour, transfer gold
leaf on gum ammoniac.

WITHIN·THE·HEART·ARE·
·UNFATHOMABLE·DEPTHS·
and THERE ARE RECEPTION ROOMS
BEDCHAMBERS IN IT· DOORS AND PORCHES
AND MANY OFFICES AND PASSAGES· IN IT IS
THE WORKSHOP OF RIGHTEOUSNESS and
OF WICKEDNESS· IN IT IS DEATH
IN IT IS LIFE·THE HEART IS
·CHRIST'S·PALACE·
THERE CHRIST THE KING
COMES TO TAKE HIS REST
WITH THE ANGELS AND THE SPIRITS
OF THE SAINTS AND HE DWELLETH THERE
·WALKING WITHIN IT AND
PLACING HIS KINGDOM THERE
THE HEART IS BUT A SMALL VESSEL
and yet DRAGONS AND LIONS ARE THERE
and there POISONOUS CREATURES and
ALL THE TREASURES OF
WICKEDNESS· ROUGH UNEVEN PATHS are there
AND GAPING CHASMS

THERE·LIKEWISE·IS·GOD

THERE ARE THE ANGELS· THERE LIFE AND
THE KINGDOM· THERE LIGHT AND THE
APOSTLES THE HEAVENLY CITIES AND
THE TREASURES OF GRACE

ALL·THINGS·ARE·THERE

LILLY LEE ADAMSON

Studio: 26 Newton Avenue, London W3 8AL, tel: 01-993 0668.

Born in USA in 1952

Member of the Chartered Society of Designers since 1986; member of Letter Exchange since 1988

Calligraphic training: Digby Stuart College, Roehampton Institute (1979-82) under Ann Camp. Crafts Council grant for further training with Donald Jackson, Sheila Waters and Richard Kindersley, 1983. Has taught at London College of Printing and West Dean College, Sussex

Recent commissions: The Crafts Council; Portsmouth City Museums; The Post Office; National Maritime Museum; South Bank Crafts Centre

Main publications: contributor to *The Calligrapher's Project Book*, Susanne Haines, *Typography-10*

Recent exhibitions: Cirencester Workshops; Stafford Art Gallery; Paperpoint, London

---

Artwork for Advertising

'Music' was a commissioned piece for a design studio, whose client was the Virgin Group, a successful entrepreneurial company in the music industry.

The booklet commissioned was for the launch of the classical selection entitled *Virgin Classics*. It was 102mm (4 inches) square in format. The designer's initial idea was to include six quotations from poems on the theme of music, interpreted by six different calligraphers, though as it happened my work was used for four of the poems.

The piece illustrated here appeared on the centrefold of the booklet and it was the only one of the four in full colour, and unretouched. The others were done in black and white, some were pasted together, others written directly. We had decided that each quotation should be executed in a different manner and style and with this idea in mind, I created a number of designs in response to each poem. From this we narrowed down our options, or the designer suggested other ideas for me to try – the teamwork was good. Timing was tight, as usual! This was one of the few commissions where I felt I had been given real artistic licence, a free rein to explore any amount of tools and colours. In fact everything that I wish a commission would be – but usually isn't!

1. One of my first attempts at creating interesting letters, using a resist method.

The first word of the chosen quotation by Confucius was 'Music', and this word was to be written across the page above the quotation itself, with the word 'Classical' dropped in above it. The designer suggested I might write each letter of 'music' in a distinctive style and string them together. I worked through a range of possible ways of doing this (**1** *and* **2**) but I still had no vision as to what I really wanted, and I doubted whether it could be pulled off successfully. I collated the various letters, written in different colours and textures, to try to get closer to the idea, as I find that physically working through something often enough can bring solutions. At this point I was writing the letters and then roughly pasting them up next to each other to see how they looked when combined – and I was following the designer's idea of 'framing' each separate letter (**3**). I realised that regarding the letters as separate entities and sticking them together in this way prevented something homogeneous and fluid from emerging, so I decided to do away with the idea of a sequence of framed letters and sit them side by side.

2. More experiments with the resist method.

3. Example of framed letter.

Yet I still had to resolve the image and make it look continuous and organic. Then, while looking at a rough where each letter had been made with a different tool (**4**), I thought of using a red coloured pencil to link them together; the last letter was written in red and red is also the colour of the Virgin Group. It worked!

In the finished piece the 'm' was written with a Coit pen, 'u' with a brush, 's' with a music pen, 'i' with a hand-made pen and 'c' with balsa wood. The rest of the quotation was written with a Mitchell pen. The word 'classical' was written separately in black and printed in colour.

4. Rough in which each letter was made with a different tool. The client liked this, and I developed it to finished artwork.

The finished piece.
Artwork for advertising
82 × 207 mm (3¼ × 8 in)
Coit pen, brush, music pen, hand-made pen, balsa wood, Mitchell pen.

Music produces a kind of pleasure which human nature cannot do without.
C O N F U C I U S

Ceramic Plaque

I am fascinated by the concept of the palindrome, a word or phrase which reads in every direction. I knew I wanted this piece to be a terracotta plaque, and I worked with a ceramicist, Richard Kindersley, who helped me with the technical matters of casting and firing.

This particular palindrome offered a challenge – if I tried to use classical capitals I would be left with unsightly gaps, and the spacing of the letters became a major concern. First came the pen stage. I tried using capitals (**1**) or minuscules (**2**) and a combination of the two (**3**, *overleaf*). I decided to stick to the design which gave me as perfect a square shape as I could obtain. From my final pen drawing I carefully traced the design off, editing as I went along, giving a flatter serif where necessary to keep the work looking solid. Joining the text from line to line was intentional, the idea being that the words should run into each other and become one (see finished piece on page 79). The letters were about 50mm (2 inches) high, written in poster pen on paper.

1. Experiment with capital letters.

2. Same exercise with minuscules.

77

3. A combination of caps and minuscules – this version is fairly close to the final design.

This image was traced onto Anchor tape, which comes from America but can be purchased in Britain. It is a malleable plastic material which unrolls, has a self-adhesive backing and can be applied onto any smooth surface; I chose to adhere it to a sheet of glass. The tape is 3-4mm (⅛ inch) thick and I used two layers, one on top of another to give an adequate depth to the letters. Had I had more time and money I would have carried on experimenting, trying out letters of different height and depth within the piece.

I then cut the image with a scalpel. The design process was still going on – I hadn't yet decided whether I wanted the letters to appear in relief or intaglio, though in the end I chose to make them relief. With the cut letters standing proud of the glass backing, it was now time to prepare a plaster cast mould. We made a square wooden frame, the shape and size we wanted the final piece to be, and covered the design with a slip, a liquid clay which makes it easier to remove dried plaster without damaging the design itself. We then placed the frame over the glass template, and poured plaster into it.

Once the plaster was dry, I removed it from the glass template – I had to be very careful as the mould was fragile. To make the letters stand really proud of

their background, I scraped and refined the design, using a potter's tool to sharpen the edge of each letter on the plaster cast. I had to use extra care as there was no turning back should I have taken too much off the edge.

If you should set out to do this type of experimental work, it is very important that you find yourself a friendly potter or an industrial ceramicist who will help you with the technical details, such as which clay to use, how much shrinkage is likely to occur between the pressing of the clay and firing, and, of course, allows you to use his or her kiln. My plaster cast actually broke in two after pressing the clay for the first plaque, but the potter was able to salvage it and press the clay for the second piece. The first plaque was left as unglazed terracotta (*see* below), and the second received a blue glaze.

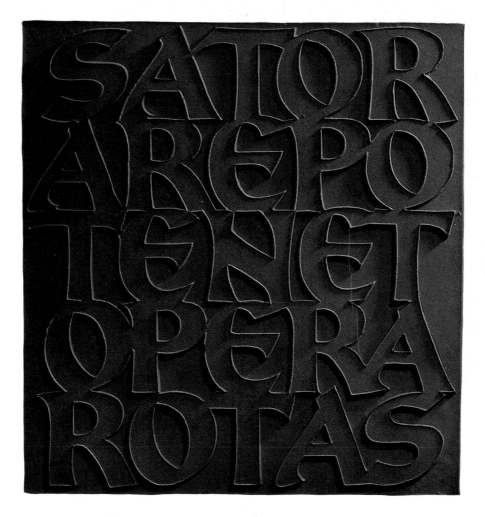

The finished piece.
'Sator Arepo', an unglazed
terracotta plaque
126 × 126 mm (5 × 5 in).

GERALD FLEUSS

Studio: 59 Chartfield Rd, Cherry Hinton, Cambridge, Cambs. CB1 4JX, tel: 0223-241224

Born in England in 1942

Fellow of the Society of Scribes and Illuminators since 1982; member of Letter Exchange since 1988 and The Art Workers' Guild since 1983

Calligraphic training: joined David Kindersley's workshop part-time in 1979. Digby Stuart College, Roehampton Institute (1981-82) under Ann Camp. Currently a part-time lecturer at Digby Stuart, where he has also run a series of workshops on heraldic design

Recent commissions: Chartered Institute of Arbitrators; College of Arms; Australia & New Zealand Bank; Greene King; Dorchester Brewery; European Heritage; GEC; Airey Neave Trust

Main publications: contributor to *The Sheaffer Book of Handwriting Styles* and *The Calligrapher's Project Book*, Susanne Haines; reproductions of work have appeared in *Modern Scribes and Lettering Artists I and II; The Calligrapher's Handbook*, ed. H. Child

Recent exhibitions: Minnesota Art Gallery; St Bride's Printing Library, London; Crafts Council; Bruges; The Spirit of the Letter, touring exhibition

Commemorative Panel – Daniel Gooch

As a child I lived in a house in Cambridge which overlooked the London and North Eastern Railway; I saw a variety of steam locomotives which sowed the seeds of my continuing passion for steam traction.

This panel celebrates the work of an early railway pioneer, Daniel Gooch, Brunel's first chief locomotive superintendent on the Great Western Railway. The initial inspiration came after a chance meeting with a man who had an interest in the life and work of Gooch. My broad intention was to chronicle the

1. First thumbnail sketch.

sequence of Gooch's designs, culminating in his magnificent 'Iron Duke' class, with its 8 ft single pair of driving wheels.

The original concept, shown in my original thumbnail sketch opposite (**1**), changed very little as the piece progressed. I wanted to emphasize the full colour painting of the Iron Duke engine and all the other elements in the design were organized to relate to the painting. A fairly detailed colour rough of the locomotive was produced as the first step. Using cut and paste technique I next put in the bulk of the text, several trials being necessary to achieve correct line spacing and an effective contrast between the various weights and textures of the writing (**2**). I then attempted to relate the small line drawings to the whole, but encountered unexpected problems in that their size and the thickness of line became highly critical in the overall scheme; about six variants were tried before a satisfactory balance was achieved.

2. One of my experiments for line thickness in the small drawings.

I wanted to incorporate the splendid Great Western Railway coat of arms into the design for its richness of colour, but my initial lay-out with the text running up to the edge of this round shape gave the upper part of the work a fragmented appearance. This problem was overcome by continuing the larger text over the coat of arms – a few trials with a complete mock-up where necessary. Gum sandarac was applied to the painted area to prevent the ink used for the writing from feathering.

'The background map, done in a light colour wash was a late addition, which helped to fill the vacuum around the central area. The last element to be considered was the heading, which was brush painted using a fine sable brush. It required several attempts, varying size and spacing, to get a good fit.

With a working rough now more or less established I made a start on the finished piece by preparing the skin (Band's manuscript vellum). Several grades of wet and dry paper were used to bring up the nap on the vellum and give a fine writing surface, whilst the painted areas were left smooth. The illustrations and small writing were then put in and since the watery colour wash of the map had unexpectedly caused heavy cockling of the skin, I decided that rather than waiting until completion, I would stretch-mount the work over 10mm (⅜ in) plywood at this stage to ensure that the larger text would come out square and true. This done, the heavier text and the

brush-painted heading were worked in and the piece completed by being framed. I took care to block the vellum away from the glass to prevent a mould developing. The green and brass colouring in the loco painting were picked up in the moulding of the frame to achieve an overall harmony. The choice of a frame can enhance but also mar the impact of a piece of work.

The finished piece. (1982) Commemorative panel. 585 × 800 mm (23 × 31 in) Stretch-mounted vellum; gouache colours and Chinese stick ink; steel pens and sable brushes.

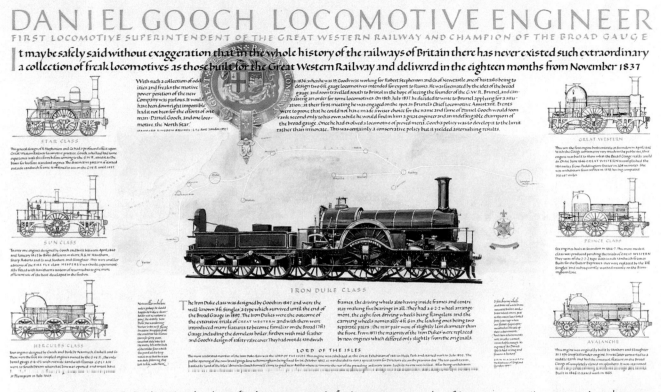

Commemorative Panel – J.F. Bentley

J. F. Bentley (1839-1902), architect of Westminster Cathedral and the leading Roman Catholic architect of his day, was my great-great uncle, and the idea for this large vellum panel, which is a sort of homage to him, had been in my mind for many years. My Gooch piece had combined calligraphy, line drawing and full colour illustrations, and I wanted to push this concept a stage further by attempting a more asymmetric treatment, with less initial planning. In the event the work took four years to complete, almost as long as the Cathedral itself!

As in the Daniel Gooch piece, I decided to establish the central colour illustration first and relate everything else to it. I find that doing this helps me to achieve an overall colour balance more easily. A fairly detailed colour rough was prepared (**1**) and the larger text, line drawings and vignettes containing the other colour illustrations were tried in different positions until a rough visual balance was achieved.

1. Detailed colour rough.

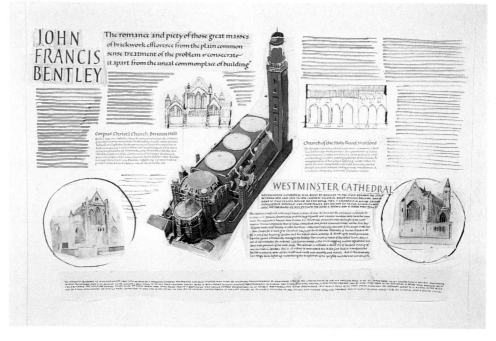

At this stage, I decided not to do any further planning, but to work, as far as possible, directly onto the final version and build up the image in the way a painter might, in an attempt to keep the whole thing fluid. The skin of vellum was exceptionally large and had to be obtained specially by the suppliers. The skin was prepared by working up a nap with several grades of wet and dry paper, pumice and gum sandarac, leaving the areas for the paintings smooth. With this completed I began work on the main illustration, which was rendered in Winsor & Newton gouache colours, with some of the shadow in watercolour or a combination of the two. Because of the scale of the painting I had to use an easel so I could step back and assess perspective, tonal contrast and so on, as the work progressed.

I next made a start on the two smaller paintings and, more or less simultaneously, the line drawings which were done in the same way as those on my Gooch piece. Later I put in their accompanying texts together with the description of Westminster Cathedral, the edges of which needed to echo the outline shapes of the paintings.

The next consideration was the larger text at the top; a few roughs were necessary to establish size, weight and spacing. With this in position I could start to fill the remaining empty spaces with the four columns of small italic writing. I chose a small lightweight text to give a subdued 'grey' background which would not conflict with the main illustration. Instead of pre-planning this stage, I wrote the whole text direct, abridging it slightly as I went along so as to finish in the right place.

The finished piece (Overleaf).
Commemorative panel (1983-86)
695 × 850 mm (27 × 33½ in)
Stretch vellum; gouache colours,
Chinese stick ink and shell gold;
steel pens and sable brushes.

One problem I hadn't yet addressed was how to fade off the cathedral at the bottom, something which was later resolved by putting in the note about the Royal Gold Medal for Architecture. Bentley was nominated for this in 1902 but died before it could be awarded.

The brush-painted main heading and subheadings were now established after a few colour trials and the final touches were the shell-gold outlines to the vignettes and gold dots on the letters of the heading. Once again, the finished panel was stretch-mounted over 10mm (⅜ inch) plywood.

Heraldic Map of Cambridge

This work was done in collaboration with Patricia Gidney and was the result of our mutual fascination with heraldry, particularly that of the Cambridge colleges. It was planned as a commercial venture, which explains the eye-catching vibrancy of the colours employed. The idea for portraying the map area itself was vague at first but was later inspired by the work of the sixteenth-century cartographer Richard Lyne, in whose 1574 map of Cambridge the notable buildings are artificially distorted in a subtle way to give them a striking prominence (**1**).

We wanted to achieve impact by placing the shields on a background whose colour would emphasize the richness of the heraldic tinctures. The first idea is shown in the thumbnail sketch (**2**). The green of the border was later abandoned in favour of a gradated blue, which together with the green of the map, gave a kind of sky and green field effect. The format was eventually changed from portrait to landscape to give a heightened drama to the work.

The first task was to produce colour roughs of the heraldry by collecting the blazons (the written description of a coat of arms) and by recording good

1. 1574 map of Cambridge, the starting point for the piece.

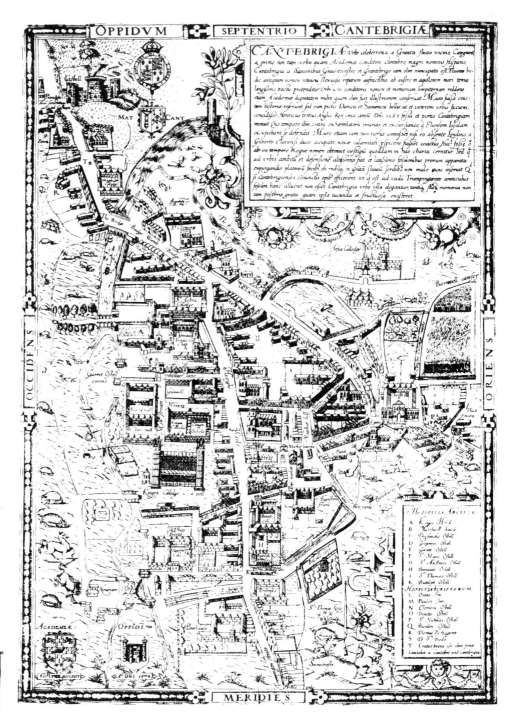

2. The first thumbnail sketch.

carved examples around the city as inspiration. When this work was complete we devised a scheme for the placement of the shields and accompanying ribbons, which was done on Fabriano paper. These, together with all other areas which were not to be painted blue, were masked off with low tack adhesive film. The gradated blue of the background of the border was then sprayed in using Winsor & Newton gouache through a Paasche V5 airbrush. When all was dry, the masks were removed and work started on the final rendering of the coats of arms, which were brush painted in gouache colours. The positioning of the arms followed a roughly chronological sequence in accord with the dates when they were granted by the College of Arms. They

3. Early rough on lay-out paper showing placement of shields, background colour and the map area using the landscape format we had now decided upon.

start with Peterhouse (founded 1284) in the top left-hand corner (*see* finished piece on opposite page) and run clockwise to Robinson (1977), with the addition of a theological college, Ridley Hall. An egg-and-dart moulding was then painted in to give a neat inner edge to the border, the outer edge of two-tone brown being intended as a sort of *trompe l'œil* wood frame.

When we proceeded to the map itself, we decided to work at a larger scale because of the intricate detail in the buildings. This part of the work was carried out on a separate sheet of Fabriano paper which could later be photographically reduced and slotted into the border section, provided the correct proportions of the rectangular shape were maintained. The topographical features were gradually painted in, again using gouache colours with a range of sable brushes. Roads were outlined with a fine-point fibre-tipped pen. The compass rose, which can make a lovely decorative addition to a map, required several trials before the colours balanced well with the heraldic colours. This, together with the cartouche containing the brush-painted title of the map, the decorative scale of miles and the little numbered indicators on shield shapes were done separately and pasted on. In order that the street names should appear finally as a dense, true black, they were pen written on a film overlay and printed separately rather than as part of the four-colour process. After trial and error, we discovered the best combination of film and ink to be double-matt drafting film with Rotring F (film) ink in an ordinary broad-edged pen. The rest of the calligraphy was done on lay-out paper, reproduced by photomechanical transfer and pasted into position on the overlay.

Finally large transparencies suitable for reproduction were made of the border/map artwork and, together with the overlay, laser scanned ready for proofing on a flat-bed proofing press. After we had made some colour adjustments the work was printed by the four-colour process on a Heidelberg Speedmaster press.

4. Early colour roughs of the shields and other elements.

The finished piece (Below).
An Heraldic Map of Cambridge
Work for reproduction: 50 × 70 cm (19½ × 27½ in)
Original artwork: border, 60 × 85 cm (23½ × 33½ in); map, 37 × 70 cm (14½ × 27½ in).
Fabriano paper, with overlays of lay-out paper and double matt drafting film; steel pens, sable brushes; Paasche V5 airbrush; non-waterproof black ink and Rotring 'F' (film) ink.
Printed by The Cloister Press, Cambridge.

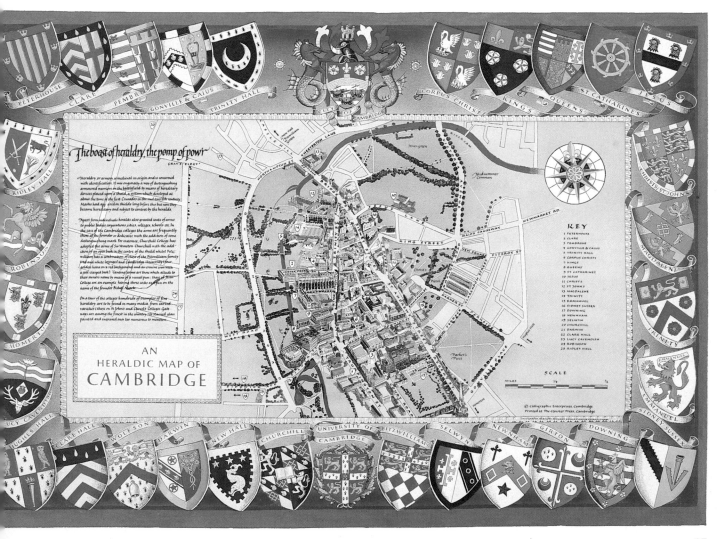

SUSAN HUFTON

Studio: 65 Derwent Crescent, Kettering, Northants NN16 8UA, tel: 0536 83518
Born in England in 1957
Fellow of the Society of Scribes and Illuminators since 1987

Calligraphic training: Digby Stuart College, Roehampton Institute (1983-86) under Ann Camp. Crafts Council Advanced Training Grant to study lettering with Tom Perkins, 1986-87. Currently an approved tutor for SSI; has taught numerous adult education evening classes

Recent commissions: British Gas; The World Wildlife Fund; London Borough of Harrow; The Schubert Society; Chenies Manor House; The Wesley Study Centre, Durham; The New Room, Bristol

Main publications: co-writer of Digby Stuart College correspondence course; contributor to *The Calligrapher's Project Book*, Susanne Haines

Recent exhibitions: London University; Chepstow Museum; Paperpoint, London

Silk and Organza Wall Hanging

The idea of the hanging initially came from drawings I made of plants, where I was looking particularly at leaf patterns and spaces. Two workable ideas sprang from parts of these studies. Patterns found in a cactus plant contained upwards and crossways movements, which suggested the possibility of three panels working together, and I was also interested in the patterns made by negative shapes of ivy leaves. The final design of the hanging evolved from a combination of these ideas.

To extend my first ideas, I used collage (**1**), marks made with an edged brush, reed pen, balsa wood, pointed brush and sponge. I then decided to use stencils and sponge and to work on the idea of negative shapes (**2**). Next I began thinking of appropriate words for use on panels and chose the poem 'Autumn in Lapland' from the writings of Dag Hammarskjöld. I had previously been working with greens but I now decided to use autumnal colours. As I was considering the use of stencilling and writing together, three aspects had to be carefully thought through:

Scale: to work successfully together, background shapes and writing must be of a compatible scale.

Strength of the background colour: this needed to be decided carefully to avoid competing with the writing or dominating it. The idea of writing on a paper overlay first occurred here, as I felt this could create interesting pattern and depth, especially if the overlay were left loose to move.

Type of writing: had to be in keeping with the mood of the piece, its meaning, shape and texture.

1. Detail of a collage of torn and cut paper exploring simple plant and cactus shapes.

2. Experimenting with stencils and sponge, using ivy leaf shapes to create negative images. As I was working on this idea I discovered the poem by Dag Hammarskjöld 'Autumn in Lapland' which is reproduced below.

AUTUMN IN LAPLAND

The warm
Rain laden
East wind
Rushes down
The dried up
River bed
   On its banks
   Yellowing birches
   Tremble
   In the storm
The opening bars
In the great hymn
Of extinction
Not a hymn
To extinction
Or because of it
   Not a hymn
   In spite of extinction
   But a dying
   Which is the hymn

The next stage involved making small thumbnail sketches to explore the arrangement of the words, as their position would affect the proportion and shape of the panels. I spent time looking at Chinese and Japanese panels and screens. Some were large structures made with up to six panels, with designs travelling right across them. I was particularly impressed by the way each panel was a successful design in itself as well as an integral part of the whole work. Simplicity was a key factor and this made the screens very powerful in their visual impact. Some used carefully repeated shapes, not necessarily stencilled but very clear and definite. Above all, careful use was made of space so that none were over-decorated.

I could have developed my ideas into the making of a screen of folding panels but I pursued the idea of a hanging. This led to thinking of the use of fabric with overlays of thin material onto which letters were painted, a possibility I found very exciting. I felt that silk would be a suitable fabric for this hanging because of its subject and design. I bought several small samples of beige and neutral coloured silks of a suitable weight for the background and a small piece of cream silk organza, fine enough for an overlay.

I started work on the background design, to decide the best positioning of the stencils so that the leaf patterns would move with the writing. I made a small pencil mock-up with the words in the intended position and lightly sketched on the areas to be leaf patterned. I collected a few beech leaves and made rubbings of the outlines (3). Then I cut a number of leaf shapes from thick paper.

3. Rubbings of beech leaves which I simplified to arrive at the stencil shapes. The two stencils also shown here still retain the paint I used for producing the wall hanging. Each stencil was used many times over across the background which is why they appear so much darker than the resultant image on the cloth.

90

I made a number of trials for the background, using the leaf shapes as stencils, and experimented with gouache paint. I was using reds, greens, browns and yellows, dipping parts of the sponge in the different colours which then mixed as I worked. I realised, however, that the colours would behave very differently on cloth, so I made some trials on calico and book cloth at this stage to see how the stencils might work on fabric.

The next stage was to design the shape of the background stencilled areas. I chose to do this on paper, where I could make changes more easily than on cloth. I made three panels of cream drawing paper and cut them to the dimensions I wanted the finished panels to be. Then, using the small pencil lay-out I had made previously as a guide, I created patterned areas of stencilled leaf shapes. I did not want an all-over leaf pattern as this would have been too heavy across three panels and not have been as visually interesting as areas of pattern moving across the panels. My aim was also to ensure that each panel in itself was balanced and visually pleasing without reference to its neighbours.

My first attempt was not right, so instead of making a completely new rough, I covered up patterned areas with pieces of cream paper. This enabled me to adjust the shape of the areas easily whilst seeing the shape as a whole. I stuck the pieces of paper down where I wanted them and did more sponging and stencilling as necessary. As I made adjustments, I frequently stood back to view the three panels together from a distance, to check that the overall design was balanced and working successfully. I eventually achieved a pleasing result and this rough became my pattern for the finished hanging.

I made three panels of lay-out paper, through which I could see the background and wrote the words faintly in pencil onto these overlays. I made adjustments until I had a rough idea of lay-out and could assess the approximate size of the letters. This rough lay-out enabled me to paint letters onto another sheet of the cream paper, of the size I wanted the finished letters to be. I painted the whole poem as a continuous piece and then cut it up into strips and laid them onto the background rough of stencilled leaf patterns, repositioning the strips until I was satisfied with the whole composition.

I designed the letters myself, basing them upon an oval skeleton 'O' appropriate to the shape of the panels. As I wanted a feeling of simplicity, the letters had no serifs but had a slight extra weighting to the ends of straight strokes to help give life and movement (**4**). The curves were weighted calligraphically – that is, the weight around an 'O' with a tilted axis being that which a pen would make, rather than weighted symmetrically around an upright axis. Calligraphically weighted letters can have a lively and contemporary feel and in this case were suited to the content and execution of the hanging.

AUTUMN
OF EXTINCTION

4. At this point I painted the letters onto paper to resolve their form.

I painted the letters onto the cream paper as if they were the finished letters because I needed to position them carefully and accurately and this would not have been possible if I had made the letters hurriedly and carelessly. Having decided on the position of the words, I was not able to follow my usual practice of sticking the strips of words down onto the background because they would have obscured a sizeable part of the patterning which I needed to see when making the finished hanging. Therefore I then carefully placed the paper overlays on top and traced the letters through, pressing more heavily on the pencil to distinguish these newly positioned letters from those previously indicated.

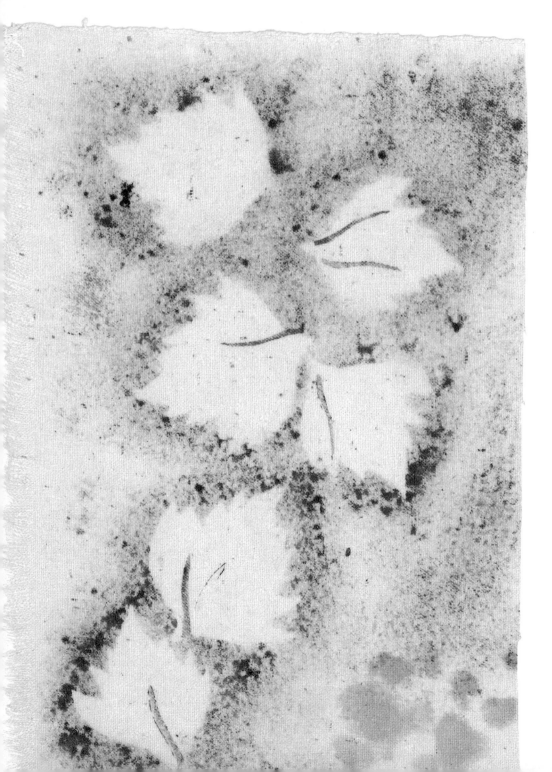

5. Experimenting with the stencils and sponge and gouache paints on the raw silk which I eventually used for the wall hanging.

The next step was to experiment with the silk samples I had bought. I liked the coloured smooth silks as they had an interesting sheen, but when I tried sponging watercolour and inks onto them the result was dull and lifeless. I concluded that the raw silk would be much more suitable for the hanging because of its weight, texture and neutral colour. The fabric was not washable so I decided to use the gouache paints I had been using in the trials (5). It should be noted that for washable fabrics, acrylic or emulsion paints can be used as they are waterproof when dry.

I soon found that I needed to keep the sponge and paint fairly dry. Paint that was too wet sank and spread into the silk and the stencilled leaves lost their definition, whereas when applied with less water the paint clung to the surface texture. Wet colours merged and muddied, drier colours stayed separate and clean. The leaf stencilled shapes looked incomplete so I tried adding veins of paint applied with a rubber stamp cut to an appropriate shape. (*See* the sample piece on the left.)

Next to the silk organza to be used for the lettering. I found acrylic and gouache too sticky for painting successfully on this. Gouache did not flow well from the brush to the surface of the silk; when the paint was too wet it blobbed, when too dry every brush mark was evident. Instead I found brown watercolour paint very good to use as it was easy to control and adhered to the silk very well. Also the watercolour letters appeared clearer and sharper when laid on top of the background than did the gouache letters. The silk organza was not washable, but I washed a small piece gently in cold water with no soap and the paint remained fast. Apart from creasing, the cloth appeared not to suffer, although I did not measure for shrinkage.

I cut the background panels to size, leaving extra for a hem at the top, and laid all three on my desk. Working with all three panels in position meant that I could see what I was doing in its entirety. I found that I constantly needed to stand back to see the panels from a distance in order to get the design right. I applied the colours as I had done in my trials by letting them mix on the cloth. Sometimes the paint was a little too wet, especially after I had dampened the sponge as necessary now and then; however, the paint did need a certain amount of dampness to adhere to the cloth. Paint that was too dry sat on the surface of the cloth and was easily smudged and rubbed. The wetter and drier areas provided variety so that the overall effect was not at all flat or regular.

The rubber-stamped veins that I had tried were not satisfactory so I decided to embroider veins onto leaves here and there. The irregularity of the embroidered lines was in keeping with the textured fabric and paint, and extra interest was added as I used a number of coloured threads akin to the gouache colours.

Finally I sewed the top hems and threaded a cane through to enable me to hang the panels on the wall and look at them across the room. Then I made final improvements as necessary until I was happy with the shape and design of the stencilled pattern.

I cut lengths of silk organza for the lettering panels wider and longer than the finished size so that I could trim them after the lettering was finished. This meant I had to take care not to let the lines run much longer than on my rough especially as I had finally decided not to trace the rough through the organza. I chose not to use any lines, guide letters or any form of help underneath or on top of the organza because I felt this would inhibit my painting of the letters. I wanted the piece to feel free and spontaneous, yet be controlled. I knew I would have to be prepared to accept lines that were not straight and a slight variation in letter size, but this would be sympathetic to the informality of the whole work.

To paint the letters I laid the organza onto my desk on top of some heavy soft paper. The slight roughness of the paper held the organza in place so no fixing or stretching was needed. Some of the paint went through the open weave of the cloth but the paper underneath soaked it up quickly. I was using fairly dry watercolour paint as the letters had to be built up slowly and carefully. Organza is a woven cloth and therefore many tiny squares of space are created; care has to be taken in order not to make 'stepped' curves. I found it best to use an 00 sable brush with a very fine point. Each letter was built up with small, short strokes – a very time-consuming operation but worthwhile as it ensured complete control.

Having painted the text in place on each panel, I worked out the place of the title exactly according to trim lines and the position of the panels alongside each other, checking them on top of the background, then I painted the words. Next I trimmed the side edges of each panel and pinned them in position at the top of the background panels. As I stood back to look at the whole piece, I was disappointed to see that the letters were hardly visible. The leaf patterns were far too prominent, something I had feared would happen as the colours were darker than I had originally intended.

The finished piece.
Silk and organza wall hanging
(1986).
920 × 1140 mm (36 × 45 in)
Raw silk and silk organza; gouache and watercolour paints; stencils and sponge; sable brushes; embroidery threads.

Suddenly I realised that I needed to move the organza overlays forward, away from the background. So I pinned a hem in the organza panels and hung them onto another cane. But the problem of legibility was not resolved. Eventually, I arrived at the solution of having another layer of organza between the letters and the background. Then I hung the canes about three centimetres apart. The background became less dominant and the letters easily readable. The hanging gained depth, becoming three-dimensional instead of two-dimensional, and moved with the air. All the problems had produced a result which was better than I had first conceived.

To finish the hanging I hemmed the two layers of organza together so that the join lay along the top of the cane and could not be seen as the piece hung on the wall. Then I frayed the side edges of the background and the overlays; fraying gave a soft edge that hung well, hemmed edges sometimes stretch and wave. Also any extra weight added with hems could have prevented the slight movements, with the wafting of air, that I wanted to happen.

I adjusted the panels so that they hung about a centimetre apart and so that the overlays were in line with the background. The panels move slightly with time and air movement because they are not fixed in any way to the canes but this is part of the character of the hanging and gives it life.

Lettering on Japanese Paper

A piece of work for me usually begins by choosing the words which then suggest methods and materials. In this case I found the reversible green and beige Japanese paper first; I liked its colour and interesting texture and then found words, again from the writings of Dag Hammarskjöld, that would be suitable. I made only one small pencil thumbnail sketch – unusual, but the quotation had given me a definite idea.

My initial idea was to have the outline of hills painted on to the paper. However, as the beige and green sides of the paper were perfectly suited to this effect, I decided to make use of both colours by tearing the hill-line and reversing the paper to form the hills. I tried out various combinations, and I decided to use the green side with the words and hills in beige. I liked the wrinkled texture of the rich green compared with the smoother beige side, and the beige hills and writing balanced well against the strong green colour.

First I painted the words in straightforward letters without serifs onto lay-out paper to determine their size, cut them into strips and rearranged them until I was satisfied with their position. I decided to use larger words for the first part of the quotation as a lead into the remaining phrases, and to create interest as well. The shape of the lay-out was also improved by these larger words. I painted the letters in beige gouache with a pointed brush; the letters had to be a reasonable weight as the creases in the paper made parts of fine strokes disappear or wobble. These were done freely onto a sheet of the Japanese paper, using several strokes to build up each letter, and allowing plenty of space for margins and mounting.

To determine the place of the tear for the line of hills, I tore a strip from another sheet of the same paper and used the beige side to lay onto the lettered sheet. I moved the strip up and down until I was happy with its position. At the same time I was using strips of card laid around the outside to indicate the margins. The hill-line and margins had to be positioned together in relation to the writing because all were interdependent.

Having decided where the hills should be I could then tear the lettered green paper in the appropriate place. I tore a strip for the beige hills from the piece I had torn off from the lettered sheet, and laid the beige strip and the

lettered piece onto another sheet of the same paper, using the cardboard strips
to check the margins again. I measured the dimensions, and was able to get a
piece of plywood to form the mount. Good plywood, made from five or more
layers of wood, remains relatively stable in changing atmospheric conditions,
and is always preferable to an inferior board.

I felt that to frame the piece in glass would obscure the texture of the paper
and some of the interest of the work would be lost. I wanted the line of hills to
lead off the edge of the piece and a frame would have 'ended' them. So I
decided to mount the piece simply on a board, letting the papers wrap around
the edges of the board.

The finished piece.
Lettering on Japanese paper
(1987).
420 × 558 mm (16½ × 22 in)

'Autumn in Lapland' and 'Humility before the Flower',
from *Markings* by Dag Hammarskjöld translated by
W. H. Auden and Leif Sjoberg are reprinted by
permission of Faber and Faber Ltd and Alfred Knopf Inc.

SHEILA WATERS

Author's photograph by Peter Waters

Studio: 20740 Warfield Court, Gaithersburg, Maryland 20879, USA, tel: 301-977-0240
Born in England in 1929
Fellow of the Society of Scribes and Illuminators since 1951; honorary member of many US
calligraphic societies, and founding president of Washington Calligraphers Guild, 1976

Calligraphic training: Medway College of Art (1947-48) under Maisie Sherley; Royal College of
Art (1948-51) under Dorothy Mahoney. Taught at Sutton & Cheam and Farnham Schools of
Art, UK, 1951-57 and at the Smithsonian Institution 1972-73. Has given workshops and
lectured in over 60 cities in USA and Canada since 1977

Commissions: Many commissions for private clients and public institutions, including an
illuminated ms. of *Under Milkwood* by Dylan Thomas for Edward Hornby; Royal Air
Force; Victoria & Albert Museum; the National Trust for Historic Preservation; The
Library of Congress. Presentation recipients include Queen Elizabeth II; Presidents Carter
and Reagan; Ansel Adams

Main Publications: 'Calligraphy', *Lettering Today*, ed. John Brinkley; 'Calligraphy in America:
a personal viewpoint' in *Calligraphy Today*; H. Child; introduction to *Creative Lettering:
Drawing and Design*, Michael Harvey; many articles and reviews for US calligraphic
journals. Recent reproductions of Sheila Waters' work have appeared in *The Calligrapher's
Handbook*, ed. H. Child; *Painting for Calligraphers*, Marie Angel; 'Profile: Sheila Waters',
Michael Gullick, *Calligraphy Review* Vol. 5, no. 1, 1987

Recent exhibitions: Guild of Bookworkers touring exhibition in USA; numerous calligraphy
exhibitions throughout USA; retrospective at Letterform Conference 1988

Roundel of the Seasons

The original calligraphic painting of 'Roundel of the Seasons' is only 256mm
(10¼ inches) in diameter, within the Ecclesiastes quotation. It was made in
1981, and from the outset it was my intention to use it as artwork from which
a limited edition of signed and numbered Cibachrome photographs would be
reproduced. It is now also available as a poster, beautifully printed in
Switzerland, twice the size of the original.

The design incorporates a kaleidoscope of motifs in rich colour and intricate
detail. Jewel-like medallions of semi-abstract zodiac symbols are interspersed
with floral decorations. A central compass point design is surrounded by
calligraphic quotations representing a sunburst and a ring of the four seasons
containing appropriate colourful motifs weaving through the painted capitals.
The colour scheme is highly intricate, an orchestration of the full colour
spectrum, with careful attention given to tonal balance. The work was
inspired by the great tradition of early miniature painting in illuminated
manuscripts. I wanted to combine imagery timeless in its significance with a
contemporary decorative feeling.

Although most of the work on the 'Roundel' was done during 1981, it was
conceived three years previously while I was completing a major project, the
production of an entirely hand-made book of Dylan Thomas' *Under Milk
Wood* (**1**). This was commissioned by the English collector, Edward Hornby.
The title-page was divided into seven horizontal bands containing the words
UNDER/MILK/WOOD/A PLAY FOR/VOICES/DYLAN THOMAS in strong capitals
painted black, outlined in white. The spaces inside and between these letters
were filled with complex imagery, suggestive of the play. The design and
colouring of these bands directly influenced my original idea of the 'Roundel'.
The action of Dylan Thomas' play is confined to a period of twenty-four
hours, opening in pre-dawn darkness and ending late at night, and the

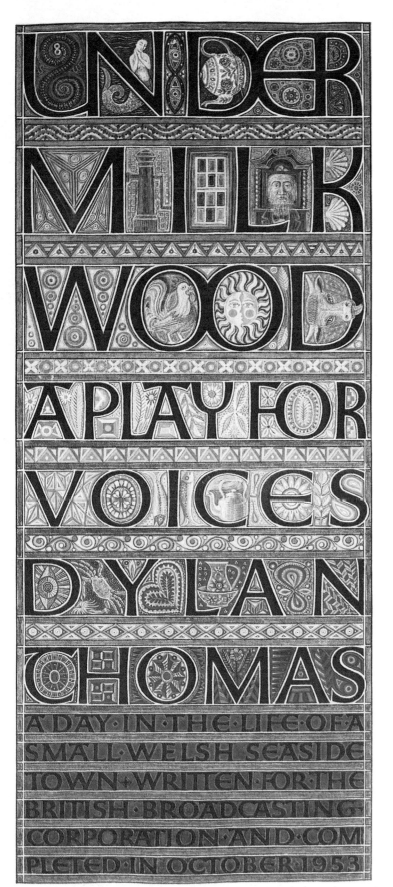

1. Title-page panel of the illuminated manuscript of *Under Milkwood* by Dylan Thomas.

progress of time was symbolized in the panel by moving through the colour wheel. While working on this panel an idea came to me which became obsessive. If the passage of the hours of a day could be presented by a vertical progression of rainbow colours, why should not a whole year be represented by a similar progression in a circle? So the 'roundel' was conceived, and I sketched a number of pencil lay-outs of my first thoughts. Because of other commitments the project was not pursued until over two years later when serious work began in January 1981.

It is thought to be the first time an artist has especially designed a work to be reproduced directly by Cibachrome, which was chosen for its proven archival qualities. Test prints were made at various stages of the work so that the colour and tonal values in the painting could be adjusted to the needs of the print medium. It quickly became apparent that because of the inherent high contrast properties of the Cibachrome photographic process, the colour intensity of the original source is reduced (colours become more muted) while tonal values expand (darks become darker, lights become lighter). So this two-way limitation had to be accounted for in the manipulation of colour and tone throughout the piece. The lighter parts of the wheel had to be darkened and the darker parts lightened to create a balanced design. The colours had to be modulated very carefully throughout the piece so that the progression would be smooth, with no individual feature 'jumping out'. For instance, blues became more muted than did other colours, so blues were intensified in the painting. I developed such a strong awareness of how the colours would be affected by the photographic process that no colour working roughs at all were made. Every colour experiment was made on the painting itself. If a colour or tone didn't work, a section was repainted until it did. I used an opaque gouache and watercolours made opaque by the addition of white gouache, so the underpainting did not bleed through and it was possible to build up successive layers of paint. In some areas, up to fifteen layers of pigment were applied, all with fine sable watercolour brushes, six of which became totally worn out during the project!

The support for the painting was fine calf-skin vellum, a natural choice because it accepts delicate calligraphy with great sharpness, stands up to repeated erasure if necessary, and is a wonderful surface on which to paint to a miniature scale. Because animal skin reacts markedly to changes of temperature and humidity by contracting and expanding, it had to be stretched over a board to keep it flat.

Even though no colour roughs were worked out, the linear design was refined many times on tracing paper. Every outline had to be clearly defined so that nothing would be left to chance (2). Once I had decided on a general scheme and the sizes and arrangements of the various elements, a geometrical under-pinning was drawn to divide the circle into twelve equal segments. The circles for the zodiac medallions were fitted into them. The zodiac symbols were chosen to represent the months because of their decorative possibilities and because they formed a unifying design element. The geometric drawing was a framework for holding the decorative detail, which was then worked out and refined in successive tracings. I carefully traced the whole outline onto the prepared surface of the vellum and picked out the geometric framework with undiluted black waterproof ink. The detailed drawing was outlined in diluted waterproof ink as the work progressed.

I first applied colour to the zodiac symbols, broadly, without detail, to set the colour wheel in progression. Then the outer ring containing the names of the months was painted in matching colour gradations. The under-pinning needed to block in the inner ring of the four seasons was completed with a fair amount of detail, and backgrounds of muted solid colour were applied to the

2. Part of the outline drawing which was traced down onto the vellum.

outer triangles which would hold the zodiac flowers. At this point, all the background was intended to be in colour – the scheme for the inner circle was quite different from the final design. The compass rose in the centre, where the colour wheel is painted, remains as intended, but at first it was surrounded by stylized flames representing the sun. Outside the ring of flames grew twenty-four leaves, chosen to fit the appropriate seasons, underpainted with a variety of greens, and with the background in sky-like blues (**3**).

3. Work in progress on the ring of leaves and the central compass rose.

This leaf/sky ring caused me a great deal of difficulty – I could find no way of adjusting the tonal values to keep the contrasts interesting, and after repainting sky, leaves and flames countless times the problems grew steadily worse. The design balance throughout the whole scheme was affected – the work looked busy, overcrowded and too dense. Several times during the work on this leaf ring, I resumed painting on the zodiac medallions where I felt on more secure ground (**4**). These, by now, were almost completed, and I had even painted in the many highlights and finalized the subtle colour modulations from one medallion to the next. I worked with the panel in an almost vertical position, and kept it covered with clear polyester film except for the area being painted.

4. Developing the zodiac medallions. At this point I was really unhappy with the centre of the piece.

Finally, because the middle simply refused to work out right, in despair I told my husband that I felt like giving it up. He looked at it for a while and then remarked wistfully, "You know, I do wish you had put calligraphy on the natural vellum background in that ring instead of those dead-looking leaves!" By that time, not only the leaves looked dead but the flames had no fire left in them, so thick was the paint! I replied "Yes, so do I, but I can't write over all that paint; I would have to scrape it all off first to get down to the vellum surface again!" "Of course," he said, matter-of-factly, though knowing full well what that labour would entail. Within ten minutes I began work on

the total erasure of the inner ring, from the edge of the frame of the seasons ring to the outer rim of the compass rose (5). This took a whole day, using sharp curved scalpel blades to scrape off the paint layers, then an electric eraser and a soft-rubber hand eraser alternately to get rid of the remaining staining. There lay the surface of the creamy-white vellum in all its perfection.

5. Erasure of the middle ring.

I thought about quotations and chose the dramatic words at the beginning of Genesis: 'The earth was without form and void and darkness was upon the face of the deep'. I decided that these would hug the compass rose in heavy black capitals. By way of contrast, the next verse springs to life: 'And God said let there be light and there was light'. These words were written in carefully modulated colours to match the progress of the colour wheel, and are also intended to represent the spectrum of refracted sunlight. I chose a flame-like calligraphic style.

The hard edge of the seasons ring needed softening, so near to it I wrote a quotation from 'Hymn to the Sun' of ancient Egypt, written in 1400 B.C.: 'Shining in the sky, a being as the sun, he makes the seasons by the months, heat when he desires, cold when he desires. Every land is in rejoicing at his rising every day.' This was done in tiny dancing orange-coloured capitals (6).

The precise fitting of the quotations needed much planning and was very exacting to do, especially the outer ring of tiny, sharp italic writing. This

6. Detail of the centre of the piece showing part of the orange lettering used for the 'Hymn to the Sun' quotation.

features the well-known passage from Ecclesiastes beginning 'To everything there is a season . . .'. The smallest size chisel-edged steel calligraphy nib was used (Mitchell roundhand no. 6) but it had to be honed to narrow its tiny width still further. Its edge was also sharpened to produce writing which was sufficiently small yet retained a clear distinction between thick and thin strokes (7).

When all the calligraphy was complete it became obvious that the inner ring and flower triangles should have been designed with natural vellum backgrounds right from the start. Interspersed throughout the circle they lighten and unify the whole scheme. The calligraphy of the inner ring provides a strong overall focus and gives more purpose to the calligraphic treatment of the outermost ring and corners. It had been very painful to wipe out many weeks of labour, but it was clear that this hard decision had been the right one. I felt, with renewed excitement, that I could now complete the project successfully.

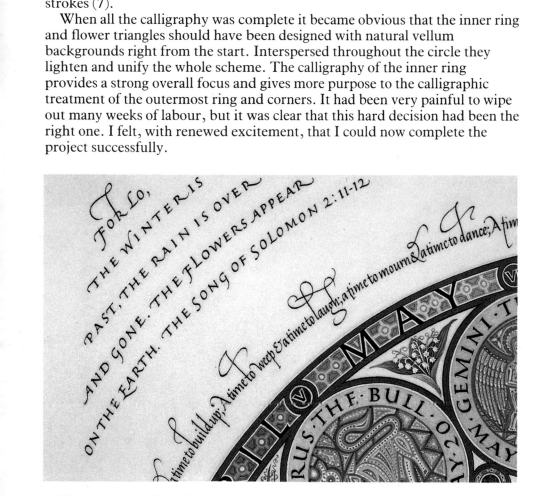

7. Detail of the italic writing used for the outermost ring and corners.

The twelve small circles, each 10mm (c. ½ inch) in diameter, which link the medallions to the seasons ring had to be filled with motifs of some kind. This had not been resolved in the planning stage, but now, when much of the work was complete, I had a novel idea – a hidden self-portrait in letters. So each of the twelve letters of 'Sheila Waters' was fitted in tiny black roman capitals in the centres of the little circles. My name and all the quotations have the same starting area, between December and January, at the bottom of the piece. The beginning of the year was a natural place to start, and it is easier to read continuous wording around a circle if it starts at the bottom, moving clockwise. (*See* finished piece on the right.)

In all, approximately a thousand hours were spent on the design and execution of the 'Roundel', the equivalent of six months' worth of eight-hour working days. My husband Peter Waters (Conservation Officer of the Library of Congress) carried out all the meticulous work of photographing and hand processing editions of Cibachrome prints in two sizes 406 × 406mm/16 × 16 inches (120% of the size of the actual painting) and 279 × 279mm/11 × 11 inches (85% of the original size). Both editions are now sold out.

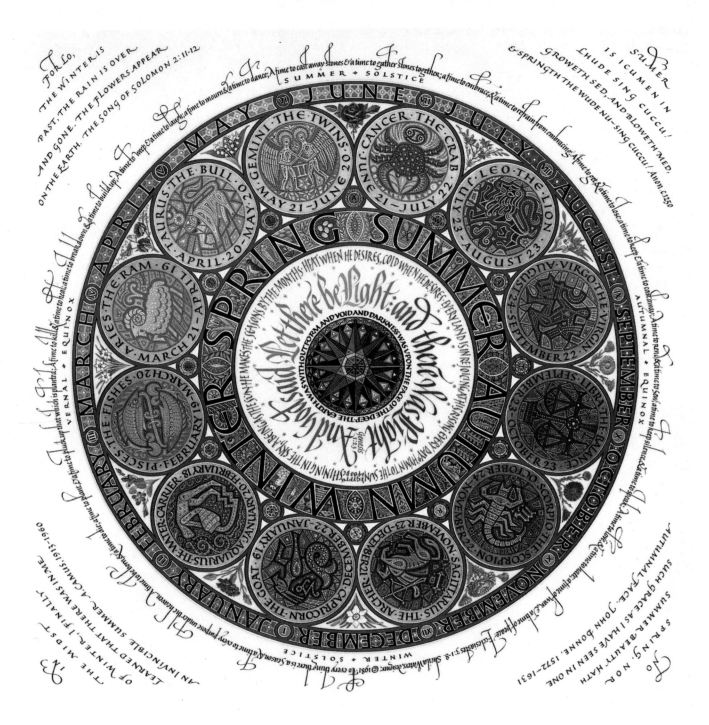

The finished piece.
The original calligraphic painting
of 'Roundel of the Seasons'
260 mm (10¼ in) in diameter
Watercolour and gouache on calf-
skin vellum.

TOM PERKINS

Studio: 40 High St, Sutton, Ely, Cambs. CB6 2RB, tel: 0353-778 328
Born in England in 1957
Member of the Society of Designer-Craftsmen, since 1978; Letter Exchange since 1988; Art and Architecture since 1986

Calligraphic training: Reigate School of Art & Design (1974-76), course on calligraphy, illumination and heraldry under Anthony Wood. 1976-77, assistant to Richard Kindersley, learning letter carving in stone and slate. Part-time lecturer at Digby Stuart College, Roehampton Institute from 1983 to 1989

Recent commissions: Peterborough Development Corporation; Mobil Oil; British Medical Association; Berkshire County Council; Cambridge City Council; the Crafts Council. Tom Perkins has also worked for Ely Cathedral and for the chapel of Magdalene College, Oxford.

Main publications: 'Calligraphy as a basis for letter design', *The Calligrapher's Handbook*, ed. H. Child; reproductions of work in *Modern Scribes and Lettering II; Lettering and Applied Calligraphy*, R. Sassoon; *Calligraphy Today*, Heathers Child; *Advanced Calligraphy Techniques*, Diana Hoare; 'Younger Generation Lettering Artists', *Calligraphic Review*, Vol 5, Nr 4, Michael Gullick

Recent exhibitions: Kettle's Yard Gallery; British Crafts Centre; RIBA Sculpture Court; Sotheby's, London

Carving Inscriptions in Slate or Stone

My usual working procedure for making inscriptions in slate and stone can be broken down into three main stages:
1 Trying out ideas on a small scale and producing a finished scale drawing
2 Drawing out the inscription full size
3 Carving, followed by painting if necessary, or gilding.

After the client has provided the wording, I first prepare a scale drawing, usually one third or a quarter of the full size. Each design has its own problems and having given thought to the wording, I consider various design ideas, I then draw out the lettering in a lay-out which is likely to be suitable (*see* sketch on opposite page). Sometimes solutions are arrived at quite quickly, but more often several adjustments will need to be made before a satisfactory result is obtained. Working on a smaller scale means that ideas can be turned around more quickly, as precise details of form and spacing are resolved in the full-size drawing. It is, however, important to make the scale drawing as accurate and informative as possible in order to convey your intention clearly to the client.

When the design has been agreed by the client (and church or cemetery authorities in the case of a headstone or memorial plaque for a church), the next stage is to order the material for the job, and prepare a full-size drawing. Stone and slate can be ordered direct from a quarry or from a firm of monumental masons. If I am to work on a circular plaque or sundial it is far more convenient to order the material circularised, as the quarry or monumental masons have the necessary machinery to do this in a fraction of the time it would take me to do it.

The full-size drawing is usually done on lay-out paper, and as before, may have to be worked over several times to get the letterforms and spacing properly resolved. If it is a centred lay-out I draw the lines for the lettering on the stone (in white crayon on slate, or pencil on a light-coloured stone), and cut out the full-size drawing into separate lines of lettering. These are centred

1. Final scale drawing for the
Paule Vezelay plaque.

on the stone and held in position with small pieces of masking tape and the
lettering is then traced down, line by line. If I am tracing onto slate I use
handwriting carbon paper; if onto stone I use a wax-free graphite paper.

Before carving, I check the inscription for spelling and punctuation, letter
by letter. For carving, I use a dummy mallet (1½ lb weight), with a circular
head made of malleable iron and an ash handle, together with a tunsten-tipped
chisel, the chisel tip being the width of the letter stem. I cut a V-shaped
incision, the depth of which depends on the size of the lettering, the type of
material, the site of the inscription and whether or not the inscription is to be
painted or gilded after carving. Slate is a good material for letter carving,
being so finely textured – the two main varieties are Welsh blue-black, and
Cumbrian greenslate. A comfortable rate of carving would be approximately

thirty to forty 37mm (1½ inch) high letters a day in slate, less in a harder stone. If it is a commission with a short deadline, the rate may have to be considerably increased.

The finished piece.
Commemorative plaque commissioned by Christopher and Sally Jarman.
457 mm (18 in) in diameter Letters incised in Welsh slate and left with natural chisel finish.

If the inscription is to be fixed in a poorly lit position it may need to be painted, with an oil-based paint, preferably with a matt finish such as the signwriter's paint 'intenso'. Slate is impervious to paint, so any painting can be done quite freely over the edges of the letters, as the inscription will subsequently be cleaned up using water and wet-and-dry abrasive paper. If gilding is required, I would use, ideally, a 24-hour gold size and loose gold leaf.

Plaques are usually fixed with concealed non-ferrous metal pins, glued with an epoxy resin into holes drilled into the back of the plaque and also glued into holes drilled on the site. If a plaque might need to be moved (for exhibitions, perhaps) I would fix brass keyhole plates into the back of it. Sundials may be raised on a stone base, which can be costly, or a brick base, though it is also possible to leave them resting on the ground, as illustrated on page 110.

As well the as technical knowledge of *how* to carve or engrave letters. I must stress how important is the fundamental ability to draw well-designed letters. Obviously, it is also important to study as much as possible about the arrangement and design of letters, but too often the letters themselves are not given sufficient consideration and are thought of as predetermined shapes or styles.

Details of full-size drawing of a plaque for Nuffield Library. (*See* finished piece overleaf.)

This stone

shorten slightly

al His Highness

Above. This detail of the drawing shows the small triangular cuts which I made in the lay-out in order to align the drawing with the guidelines on the slate.

When we draw a letter on paper without reference to an exemplar, we are communicating our understanding of a particular letterform. A successful letter depends on a clear view of how the various parts combine to make a harmonious whole. Without this awareness it is of little use acquiring the technical ability to carve letters or engrave them on glass. These words by Percy Smith, a calligrapher and letterer, from his book *Civic and Memorial Lettering*, give sound advice for the beginner or anybody wishing to improve their letterforms: 'Any organised scheme of training may well include a little time given to the making of full-size pencil studies of good letters. Such studies can be a means of developing a sense of what is noble in proportion and of discovering subtle and beautiful details, points not to be despised by students in any branch of the arts. And to draw letters, entirely freehand, with a sharp pencil-point is also excellent training towards mastery of precision, a quite valuable, though relatively incidental, accomplishment.'

The finished piece.
Plaque commissioned by the
British Medical Association.
457 mm (18 in) in diameter
Letters incised in Welsh slate.

Generally speaking my working methods remain very much the same which is why I have not attempted to describe the way each individual piece was designed and executed. The name plate for Barry Urquhart Associates that follows is a fairly typical example of commissioned work. The sundial and the glass bowl are types of commissions I undertake less frequently.

1. Scale drawing of a plaque for an architectural practice, as sent to the client.

(2)

(3)

2-4. Various details of full size drawing.

(4)

BUA *Barry Urquhart Associates* CHARTERED ARCHITECTS

Engraved Glass Bowl

As this was one of my first attempts at engraving letters on glass, I deliberately selected a bowl with fairly straight sides, as it would be more difficult to design for a bowl which tapers. A short inscription was selected, which enabled me to keep the letters reasonably large. Trying to work too small can cause problems if you have little experience of glass engraving, as small-scale letters do require more skill to engrave.

It was fairly straightforward to ascertain the circumference of the bowl by wrapping a piece of lay-out paper round it. Once the design had been worked out on paper, I prepared the bowl for engraving in the following way. The surface of the glass was coated with white poster paint, applied with a broad chisel-edged brush. When the paint had dried, the inscription was transferred from lay-out paper to the glass by placing a sheet of handwriting carbon paper between the lay-out paper and the bowl, and going over the letters with a hard (4H) pencil. Before taping down and tracing, I had to take great care to make sure the lettering was in exactly the right position on the glass.

The engraving was done using an electrically-powered dental drill, with a flexible drive and small spherical burrs. It is useful to have a selection of these for different sizes of lettering and a few pointed ones for getting corners sharp, and so on. I prefer to engrave the letters from the centre of the stroke towards the edges, rather than outlining and filling in. The former method leaves you free to modify the contours of the letter as you go along.

After I had worked on the letters as far as was possible through the white paint, the paint was washed off under running water. With a dark cloth inside the bowl to give a good contrast, the letters underwent a final refining process; close attention was paid to defining the edges clearly and the relative weights of stems and curves were adjusted so that each letter was of a uniform weight.

The finished piece. (Left) Plaque for an architectural practice, commissioned by Barry Urquhart Associates. 152 × 825 mm (6 × 31½ in) Letters incised on dark grey slate and painted off-white.

The finished piece. (Left) Portland stone sundial, 510 mm (20 in) in diameter. Letters incised and left with a natural chisel finish. Quotation reads: 'The sun with one eye vieweth all the world'.

The finished piece. (Right) Engraving on Orrefors glass bowl. 190 mm (7½ in) in diameter. Quotation reads: 'The kindly fruits of the earth'.

GAYNOR GOFFE

Studio: 40 High St, Sutton, Ely, Cambs. CB6 2RB, tel: 0353-778 328
Born in England in 1946
Fellow of the Society of Scribes and Illuminators since 1978; member of Letter Exchange since 1988

Calligraphic training: Reigate School of Art and Design (1975-78), Surrey Diploma in calligraphy, illumination and heraldry under Anthony Wood. Assistant to Donald Jackson, 1979-81. Has taught widely at residential colleges, and is a part-time Lecturer at Digby Stuart College, Roehampton Institute since 1983

Recent commissions: The Craftsmen Potters' Association; Golgonooza Press; International Sacred Literature Trust; the Post Office; Michael Peters Group

Main publications: contributor to *The Calligrapher's Project Book*, Susanne Haines; reproductions of Gaynor Goffe's work have appeared in *The Calligrapher's Handbook*, ed. H. Child; *Lettering and Applied Calligraphy*, R. Sassoon; *Modern Scribes and Lettering Artists II*; *Calligraphy Today*, Heather Child; *Advanced Calligraphy Techniques*, Diana Hoare; *Calligraphy Review*, summer 88

Recent exhibitions: SSI exhibitions 1981-89; Paperpoint, London; Guild of Devon Craftsmen

Alphabet Design

This piece grew out of some spare time spent experimenting. My first idea was to write a large-scale, heavy-weight alphabet in capitals, with a vertical lay-out and very little white space within or between letters or lines. Initially, I tried Roman capitals with an automatic pen, using a 12.5mm (half inch) wide nib, with letters 32mm (1¼ inches) high (**1**). As I wanted a long narrow column, I decided to try laterally compressed capitals with the same pen; these were 75mm (3 inches) high, and four or five letters per line, with a broken texture created in strokes written fairly rapidly on lay-out paper (**2b**). The original idea was for the letters to be solid black, but I decided to take advantage of the broken effect and accept it as part of the design. I then tried an even more compressed alphabet (**2a**). This version happened to come out with less textured strokes, which was also an acceptable effect. I decided to write several alphabets on different papers to see what variety of stroke textures the paper surfaces would give. This was also affected to some extent by the degree of pressure on the nib, and the amount of ink in the nib. The number of letters per line and amount of lateral compression varied slightly in this series, as it was an experiment.

Having written about twelve alphabets, I thought a contrast of weight, scale and movement was needed to enhance the design and I tried some quickly written lightweight flourished capitals with a thin nib on lay-out paper. I found I could not write them quickly enough to get the movement I wanted at this large scale (the letters were approximately 50mm/2 inches high) – there was too much resistance between the edged nib and the paper. So I tried writing them with the corner of the automatic pen, which worked much better, enabling flow and speed. I wrote several sheets of these lightweight flourished capitals in ink, to get used to the movement (*see* page 114). I decided on blue-grey gouache to give the effect I wanted on top of the large black alphabet column, and I wrote as many flourished capitals per line as were required to cover the column width and overlap somewhat at the sides. I also tried some rust-red and yellow capitals over the heavy black alphabet columns and experimented with different sizes of light flourished capitals ranging from 19-64mm (¾ to 2½ inches) on final versions. I preferred the

1. First rough of the large-scale, heavy-weight alphabet.

112

larger size capitals, as the smaller ones made the whole panel look too busy.

I had written on some pale blue and grey papers as well as on white, and felt the designs on the coloured papers would be improved by the addition of a second lightweight flourished alphabet in white. These were written somewhat offset from the previous underlying light capitals. On the white sheets of paper I added the further lightweight flourished alphabet in yellow or rust overlaying the blue-grey ones. All the light alphabets were written standing, as a considerable amount of arm movement was required.

2a and **2b.** Experiments with
  compressed capitals written
  with an automatic pen.

(2a)   (2b)

3. Experiments with light-weight flourished capitals written with the corner of an automatic pen.

One or two of the versions were spoilt by blobs and spatters (although other versions did not seem spoilt by these), and I added some pen diamonds as a further decorative element to try to salvage two or three of the panels. I then added pen diamonds to a number of the other panels too, though some I preferred without.

This series was completed quickly, and I enjoyed being able to experiment and make adaptations as I went along, having no constraints as to the look of the final design.

The finished piece. (Right)
Alphabet design.
620 × 500 mm (24 × 19½ in)
Paper; ink and gouache; automatic pen.

114

Calligraphic Panel

This was a commission for a panel of calligraphy, where I was free to select the text. I took some excerpts from an article written by Kamaladevi Chattopadhyah in *Resurgence* magazine, which I had previously collected with an idea of making a large panel, and I regarded this commission as a step towards that aim. I selected what seemed to me a key statement, one which I wanted to dominate this piece of work and to be fairly large-scale. I wrote this in a formal italic in a Rexel 1½ roundhand nib, as I thought formality suited the content of the quotation; I wanted a minuscule hand and I particularly like writing italic. I decided on an interlinear space of approximately one and a half 'x' heights, to contribute to the classical look I wanted for the main area of text. This proved an adequate space as the italic was laterally compressed. A closer interlinear spacing would have made the text look too busy whereas wider spaces between the lines would have weakened the overall look of the block. I tried the word 'craft' in larger italic, Roman and compressed capitals, to give more dominance to it as a significant introductory word, and chose the slightly informal Roman capitals.

I selected a few further excerpts which I wished to include, and tried one in a line of small Roman capitals placed above the main italic block as a contrast to it. Bearing in mind the length of the quote and that I wanted it to stretch across the width of the panel, I tried one or two smallish-sized nibs and settled on a Rexel 4. I wanted an open texture for the capitals as a contrast to the narrow italic, and a slight forward slope to give them some movement. I then needed a line of text across the bottom of the panel, to balance with the line of small capitals at the top yet to be different from them and to make sufficient contrast with the large italic. I tried small cursive italic, first in quick handwriting and subsequently in a slower cursive. I included some flourishes to offset the formality of the main block, designing several and pasting them onto the small italic until I got a satisfactory line.

Although the subject matter required a formal treatment, I also wanted a less formal element included in the panel. As I did not want a title across the top, I thought an alphabet might be appropriate, and would give plenty of

1. This was the only rough I made before completing the piece. On the rough I pasted new lines of writing over earlier ones as I refined the design concept.

ABCDEFGHIJKLMNOPQRSTUVWXYZ

WHAT SURVIVES IS ESSENCE IN TRADITION IT IS THE ESSENCE OF THE MILLENNIA SINCE LIFE CAME TO BE

CRAFT means cultivation of an intimacy with human life
a sympathy for all living things and creation,
and the realisation of the fundamental unity
of all aspects of life though diverse in form

FROM
CRAFTS & THE FUTURE '
BY KAMALADEVI
CHATTOPADYAH

Tradition is all pervasive and touches human life at every phase it can never be broken   Tradition is the seed from which life always blossoms

scope for various treatments. I wanted the letters to be fairly large and freely written, to tie in with the rest of the design yet contrast with the dominant element – the large italic – so I decided to try Roman capitals with an element of freedom in them. I wrote these in the same nib as the large italic and at the same height as the capitals used for the world 'Craft'. This seemed all right and I did not experiment further, using them on the final piece. Initially they were spaced closely, creating too solid a line across the page, so I spread them further apart and added pen-made diamond shapes and crosses between the letters, using gum ammoniac. These shapes were gilded with transfer gold. Different colour schemes were tried; I began by alternating purple and blue capitals, but these looked too strong; subsequently I used more muted colours, milky-green and grey/blue, which I retained. I inserted the source of the quotations and author's name on the left in small Roman capitals to link up with the other areas of Roman capitals, as shown on the rough (**1**).

I did not make any preliminary pencil lay-outs; this piece grew from the central italic block, I ruled up and worked on three pieces to the same design, which enabled me to enjoy writing the pieces more freely (*See* finished piece below.) I used powdered gum sandarac rubbed into the Chatham Vellum paper to increase the sharpness of the writing. In the event, the panel turned out much larger than the client wanted and I started something completely different!

The finished piece.
Calligraphic panel.
394 × 610 mm (15½ × 24 in)
Mould-made paper; pens; ink and gouache.

ABCDEFGHIJKLMNOPQRSTUVWXYZ

WHAT SURVIVES IS ESSENCE IN TRADITION IT IS THE ESSENCE OF THE MILLENNIA SINCE LIFE CAME TO BE

CRAFT means cultivation of an intimacy with human life a sympathy for all living things and creation, and the realisation of the fundamental unity of all aspects of life though diverse in form

FROM
'CRAFTS & THE FUTURE'
BY KAMALADEVI
CHATTOPADHYAH

Tradition is all pervasive and touches human life at every phase it can never be broken ⌇ Tradition is the seed from which life always blossoms

Poster

I worked on this commission with Tom Perkins, my husband, as the time-scale was very short. We were given a size to work to 425 × 1190mm (16¾ × 46¾ inches), landscape format. There being no time for rough designs, we worked full-size from the start to provide paste-up camera-ready artwork, designing it as we went along. We were provided with the quotations by the clients, the Michael Peters Group, and it was suggested that a fairly formal calligraphic look was required, with legibility as a priority.

Due to teaching and other work commitments, we had two days each (including nights!) to work on the commission. I spent one day evolving the core of the design. I chose two quotes of medium length which could be written fairly large, and which particularly appealed to me. Within the constraints of legibility, and the fact that no overlays could be used (as we did not have time to consider this possibility), I wanted a reasonably informal lay-out. I thought the quote about rainforests suggested there be a rhythmical quality in the writing, and tried this in an informal italic in three sizes, settling in the end for a Rexel 1 roundhand nib (**1**). I then wrote it more carefully and pasted it onto a background sheet, offset to the right side of the centre, breaking it into line lengths I thought suitable, and aligned left.

1. First idea for main text block.

We are fighting to defend the forest.
It is because the forest is what makes us,
and makes our hearts go. Because
without the forest we won't be able to breat
and our hearts will stop
AND WE WILL DIE

PAULINO PAIAKO & KUBE-I

It seemed that the panel needed an even stronger visual core, but I did not want to change the area I had just written. I decided to isolate a shorter but vital quote, or part of one, to be written larger, and selected 'No second Noah's Ark'. I tried this first in Roman capitals with a large automatic pen, but it looked too calm and unnoticeable for an area I wanted to focus on, so I tried compressed capitals which gave a more dynamic appearance. I wrote some versions on lay-out paper in solid black ink (**2**) and some on rough paper to give a textured effect, which was finally used on the artwork. The large italic rainforest quote was rearranged so the line beginnings fitted round the central core. I had in mind a strong block of italic and settled on an interlinear space of approximately one 'x' height, which was adequate as the italic was narrow. I wrote the final phrase in the same nib in Roman capitals, for emphasis.

With these two elements in position I had to narrow the loop of the flourish at the beginning of the italic quote so it did not overlap with the central quote, as we were not including overlays for colour separation but having to paste all text up on one sheet. This resulted in the flourish looking more cramped than I wanted, but I had to leave that to move on with the rest of the design.

I made a start on the left side of the poster, trying a block of smaller Roman capitals with close interlinear spacing, in an attempt to fill in a further area of the overall design, even though I was not sure that this would work without several tries with different styles, weights and textures of letters.

2. Trial for central quote with
untextured strokes.

NO
SECOND
NOAH'S
ARK

MIKHAIL

GORBACHEV

The next day Tom worked on the lay-out. He decided we should try a quote
along the top and bottom of the panel to bind it together laterally. He tried
large automatic pen Roman capitals for the top (*see* overleaf **3**) but these were
overpoweringly large and created a conflict with the compressed capitals in
the centre of the panel. He then tried Roman capitals to match the size of
those used for 'AND WE WILL DIE', and this was more successful, so we pasted
this on (**4**). I then wrote out the names of all the authors of the quotations in
small Roman capitals and a further quote in italic to go across the bottom of
the panel. Initially this was a very compressed italic, but it looked too dense,
so was written again to make it look more open; two or three nib sizes were
tried to get a suitable length of line which would stretch the panel width. We
continually pinned the paste-up on the wall to stand back and assess the
overall design before deciding on styles, sizes and weights of lettering we
would try for additional areas of text.

WE·ARE

IT TO BE WRECKED

THERE WILL BE

3 and 4. Two sizes and styles of
capitals tried for the top of the
poster by Tom Perkins.

It is because the forest is what makes us,
and what makes our hearts go
Because without the forest

5. Detail of the main italic block.

We then had four quotations left to incorporate in the panel, in the areas to right and left of the central core. We decided to juxtapose small or medium-sized Roman capitals and italic for contrast, not wishing to introduce too wide a range of scripts as time in which to experiment was very limited. Tom wrote a quote in italic for the left side, but then thought one of us should write all the italic and the other the Roman capitals to keep some similarity within these two styles, so I re-wrote the italic quote and Tom re-wrote the authors' names. He then tried one or two different weights and sizes of Roman capitals for two further quotes (**6**).

SCIENTISTS AND LAWYERS PREFER THE TERM
'MARINE POLLUTION', HIGH-SOUNDING WORDS
DERIVED FROM LATIN, A COMMON EUPHEMISTIC
TRICK TO SOFTEN UNPLEASANTNESS OR CONFER
RESPECTABILITY....

ARE POISONING AND POLUTION
TWO DIFFERENT THINGS? OR IS THE DIFFERENCE
ONLY A CHOICE OF WORDS?

6. First try out of capitals by Tom Perkins.

Tom had one more day to finalize everything on the artwork. The remaining long quote by Barbara Ward had to be written small, and we felt italic would be suitable in the context of the overall design. Tom wrote the final quote in a small cursive italic, which did not conflict visually with all the larger italic I had written. Disaster struck when I came to clean up the paste-up. I had run out of my favourite ink and had to use a different one, which smudged when I rubbed away the surplus cow gum – I ruined the large italic block and had to re-write it at 2 a.m.!

Although we were not able to consider overlays of texture and colour because we did not have time, the clients decided when the artwork was delivered that some large flourishes should be added on an overlay to unite the poster laterally, so I added these 'on site' using some textured paper to give a broken effect to the strokes, matching the rough-textured centre preferred by the clients. The central quote in capitals and additional flourishes were pasted up once more on an overlay.

I had given considerable thought to colour schemes, but fortunately the clients were willing to devise this, and the posters were printed in six muted colours on re-cycled paper. Working out the relative sizes, weights and textures of lettering in black and white with no colour trials is not ideal when the final article is to be printed in several colours, but it is an approach one often has to adopt in the world of deadlines. (*See* finished piece below.)

The finished piece. (Below)
Poster commissioned by the
Michael Peters Group (1988).
425 × 1190 mm (16¾ × 46¾ in)
Printed in six colours on recycled
paper.

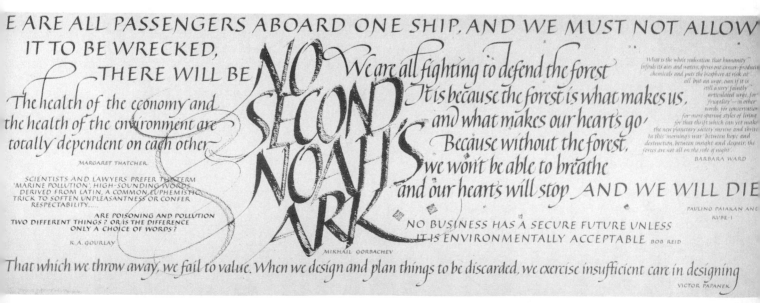

PETER HALLIDAY

Author's photograph by Alan Ginman

Studio: 26 Stapenhill Rd, Burton-on-Trent, Staffs. DE15 9AE, tel: 0283-68320
Born in England in 1939
Fellow of the Society of Scribes and Illuminators since 1976; founder member of Letter
    Exchange, 1988

Calligraphic training: Medway College of Art (1956-60) studying writing, illuminating and
    lettering with Maisie Sherley. Part-time lecturer in calligraphy at Burton-on-Trent Technical
    College. Has taught numerous workshops in UK, Europe and USA; External Examiner for
    certificate, diploma and advanced diploma in calligraphy and bookbinding at Digby Stuart
    College.

Recent commissions: has worked on numerous commissions for private clients

Main publications: introductions to *Modern Scribes and Lettering Artists II*; *Calligraphy in Print*
    catalogue and *Calligraphy 84*. Reproductions of Peter Halliday's work have appeared in
    Contemporary British Lettering; *The Calligrapher's Handbook*; *60 Alphabets*, Gunnlauger S.E.
    Briem; *The Calligrapher's Project Book*, Susanne Haines

Recent exhibitions: SSI exhibitions 1977-89; Master Eagle Gallery, New York; Whitworth
    Gallery; '60 Alphabets', touring Europe and USA; Maine Coast Artists' Gallery, Rockport,
    USA; Ruskin Gallery, Sheffield City Art Gallery; Rufford Crafts Centre

Three-dimensional Calligraphic Composition

E.E. Cummings was a New England poet of lyrics and satires, who was also a painter of some accomplishment. He once described himself as 'an author of pictures, a draughtsman of words'.

It may well be Cummings' attention to the visual nature of his poetry which first attracted me to his work. Much of it was designed on the typewriter, where he altered the emphasis of words by a novel juxtapositioning of upper and lower case letters. He repositioned words, and parts of words, and by doing so often seemed to distill his subject-matter to its essence – but not always in the most obvious of ways.

My response, calligraphically, to his work represents a departure from the more traditional notions of calligraphy as a craft. In some of my interpretations of his work the concept and process have become more important than the calligraphy. The *meaning* of the words has taken over. This seems to me to be consistent with the employment of calligraphy as an interpretive medium: more caligraphic 'art' than 'penmanship'.

George Firmage, an authority on Cummings' work, says that this poem 'is a play on "one" and "self-ness" – the letter "l" also acting as the arabic numeral "1" on most typewriters – as well as a visual image of "loneliness" in the picture of "a leaf falls".' He goes on to say that Cummings probably 'had in mind an autumn leaf (red, yellow, brown), being a good New Englander well acquainted with what is known in the States as "Indian Summer"'. Indeed, on visiting Cummings' summer home in Silver Lake, New Hampshire, I was interested to see a summer-house in the woods nearby; his housekeeper, Mrs Shackford, told me he would sit there for long periods of time contemplating the surroundings – perhaps considering this poem.

The alignment and spacing of the poem, as Cummings originally laid it out, is something which I was not at liberty to alter and a constraining feature which affected my interpretation.

Below. The poem by E.E. Cummings.

l(a

le

af

fa

ll

s)

one

l

iness

I decided that both the visual idea of the leaf falling, and the significance that takes on could be conveyed by a combination of drawing and symbolic colour. The swirling movement, suggestive of the path of the falling leaf on a still and silent day, might be visually connected with the layout of each line. Yellow and purple were used as complementary colours, each modified and mixed as pale tints, which to me symbolized the poem's feeling of alienation and separation.

1. The original concept. It shows how the sketch grew around the cut-out corner of the scrap of paper. At that stage I felt that the colours used were too strong and dominated the text completely.

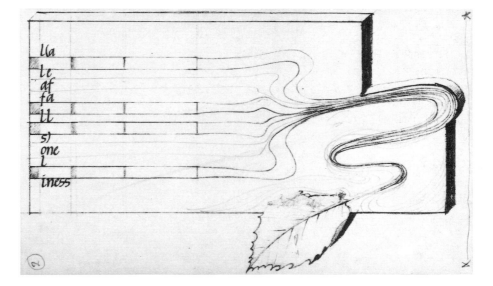

2. A careful drawing of the early concept which included perspex and a three-dimensional cut-out shape.

The initial design idea (1) was drawn out on some scrap paper which happened to be to hand. This paper had a piece cut out of it, which became significant later although initially it did not play a part in the design developments. As can be seen from the careful drawing out shown in (2), at this stage I considered using a layer of perspex (Plexiglass) and also thought about the possibility of a three-dimensional cut-out shape against an unframed background. (I had earlier experimented with similar ideas with other works of Cummings.) This stage was followed by a process of evaluation and the

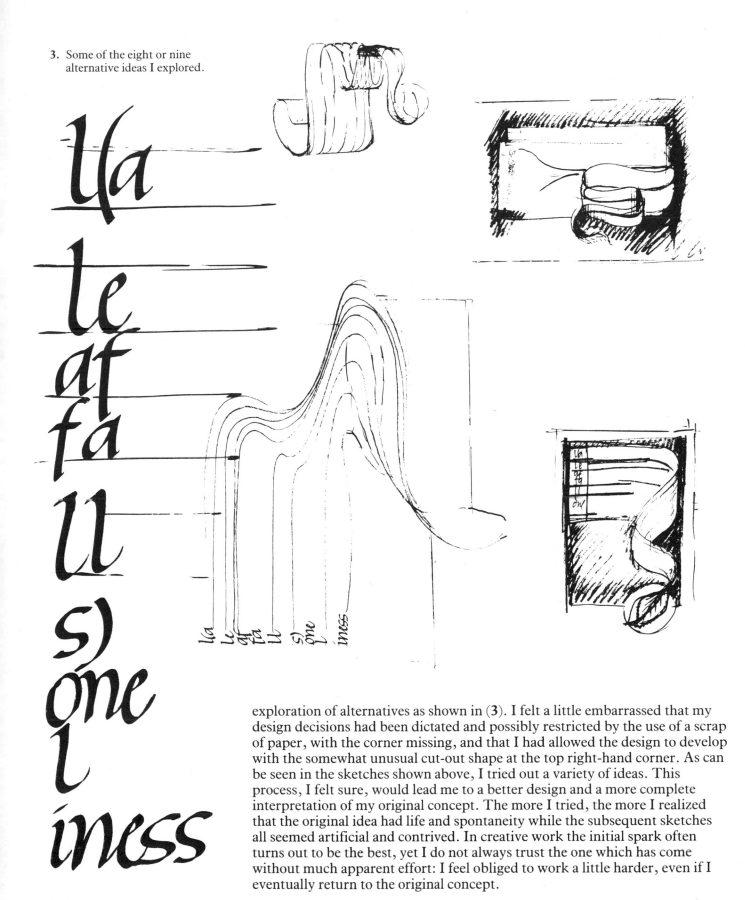

3. Some of the eight or nine alternative ideas I explored.

exploration of alternatives as shown in (**3**). I felt a little embarrassed that my design decisions had been dictated and possibly restricted by the use of a scrap of paper, with the corner missing, and that I had allowed the design to develop with the somewhat unusual cut-out shape at the top right-hand corner. As can be seen in the sketches shown above, I tried out a variety of ideas. This process, I felt sure, would lead me to a better design and a more complete interpretation of my original concept. The more I tried, the more I realized that the original idea had life and spontaneity while the subsequent sketches all seemed artificial and contrived. In creative work the initial spark often turns out to be the best, yet I do not always trust the one which has come without much apparent effort: I feel obliged to work a little harder, even if I eventually return to the original concept.

4. At this stage I have almost arrived at an acceptable colour scheme.

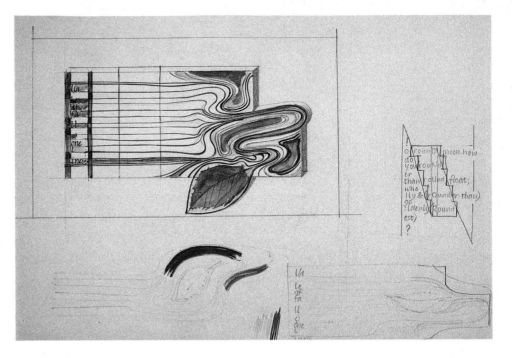

Eventually I arrived at the idea sketched out in (**4**) here I decided to split the central panel, intending this to symbolize the loneliness of a person peering out from behind curtains. The final design was then drawn out and at this point the cut-out shape was reintroduced. The calligraphy was rehearsed and a RWS hot-pressed paper was selected.

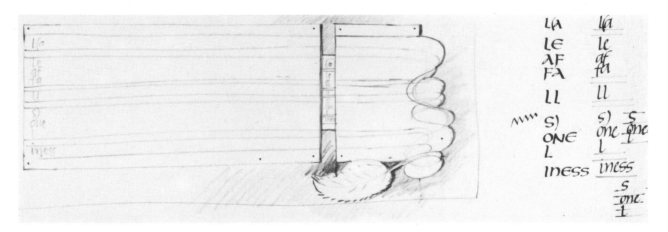

5. The finalised drawing.

The final version was made in the following order:
1) the calligraphy was written
2) the design drawn out and traced on to paper
3) the leaf was drawn directly from one picked up from the garden
4) the straight lines were drawn in colour with a ruling-pen
5) the flowing lines painted with a brush and the other areas painted in
After careful tracing had been made of the finished version, the perspex was cut out and polished, and the same shape cut out from plywood. Both were then cut in the place where the design was split. The smaller repeated version of the poem was fitted into place – it was set into the background surface, which had already been painted with several layers of black emulsion paint modified with the addition of PVA medium. Lastly, the pieces were carefully drilled from behind and screwed together. (*See* finished piece overleaf.)

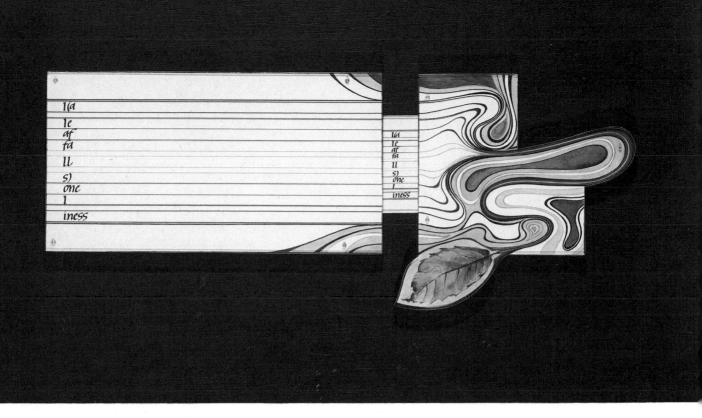

Calligraphic Panel

Many artist-craftsmen who sell their work to the public, or by commission, say that they would like to chose their clients with more discrimination. After all, the client is buying a little piece of the maker.

"The Cherry Tree' was a commission for a personal friend of many years standing as a retirement present from his fellow colleagues. He chose the poem, after much thought and consideration, but was not to see the completed work until it was presented.

I knew that he appreciates the kind of work which I produce, but there was no guarantee that he was going to like this one. I was quite happy for him to be the recipient of 'a little piece of the maker', and I set to work with him in mind – not to do the piece in a particular way because I thought that he would like it but it did develop as if he were looking over my shoulder.

Inspired by a magnificent cherry tree in my own garden, which is smothered with bloom every spring, I decided to use formalized imagery as a background to the poem. The blossom, when caught by the wind, blows like a snow storm across my lawn and this imagery seemed appropriate for the backdrop. The first design idea was carried through almost unchanged in concept. The choice of paper, creation of the backdrop and the actual making of the piece posed a much bigger problem than arriving at the concept itself. I wanted to use soft paper which is difficult to write on because the sensitivity required would have a profound effect on the script. I looked out some Japanese paper from my store of 'waiting paper' – waiting for a job to come along which is just right for it – and found some deep burgundy coloured paper, soft and sensitive. I knew this would need some preparation – I

The finished piece. (Above)
Three-dimensional calligraphic composition.
295 × 474 mm (11½ × 18½ in)
Gouache, ink on paper; perspex, plywood; black emulsion.

envisaged burnishing it with a smooth pebble to make the surface smoother without seeming to alter the particular appearance of the paper. I managed to achieve this effect on a trial piece. I had an idea as to how I wanted to handle the background, inspired by traditional Japanese stencil cut designs. Such designs, printed on silk and cotton, involved remarkably fine and complex cutting and the use of punches. This seemed to be an ideal starting point for my background. So, using a scalpel and an old, large hole punch I devised the design and cut it through, a process which proved to be very intricate and time-consuming. It was, however, most effective when laid over 6mm (1¼ inch) plate glass, under which I had laid some off-white Japanese paper. Changes of light and the position and movement of the viewer enhanced the effect of mutability. On the burgundy surface, along with the writing and also on the off-white under paper. I placed small spots of gold to coincide with the cut-outs and to add sparkle to the formalized 'snow storm', and these also vary with the light and movement of the viewer.

The writing was done using Chinese white watercolour which allowed the paper's colour to show through very slightly and it was written with a quill, the most sensitive kind of pen and one which could be cut specifically for the purpose. The small spots of gold were pushed into the soft paper with a burnisher to keep the gold away from the glass and to allow them to shine.

It is pleasing to note that on the day of the presentation the recipient seemed very pleased with the offering and later, with my assistance, carefully chose a position for hanging the piece to gain the best advantage of the changing light throughout the day.

1. The original design idea which was carried through, virtually unchanged.

The finished piece.
Calligraphic panel. The Cherry Tree from *A Shropshire Lad* by A.E. Houseman.
190 × 710 mm (7½ × 28 in)

Japanese paper; watercolour – Chinese white; transfer gold on PVA medium; quill.
In the collection of Mr B.W. Morgan.

BIBLIOGRAPHY

Techniques
Painting for Calligraphers, Marie Angel (Pelham Books/The Overlook Press, 1984)
Pen Lettering, Ann Camp (A & C Black/Taplinger, 1984)
The Practical Guide to Lettering and Applied Calligraphy, Rosemary Sassoon (Thames & Hudson, 1985)
Writing, Illuminating and Lettering, Edward Johnston (reissued of 1906 edition, A & C Black/Taplinger, 1983)
The Calligrapher's Handbook 2nd edition, Heather Child, editor (A & C Black/Taplinger, 1985)

History
The Illuminated Manuscript, Janet Backhouse (Phaidon, 1979)
A Book of Scripts, Alfred Fairbank (Faber, 1979)
The Story of Writing, Donald Jackson (Studio Vista/Taplinger, 1981)
Historical Scripts, Stan Knight, (A & C Black, 1984)

Compilations
Modern Scribes and Lettering Artists II, Ieuan Rees and Michael Gullick (Trefoil/Taplinger 1986)
The Calligrapher's Project Book, Susanne Haines (Collins/Crescent, 1987)
Lettering Arts in the 80s (Ampersand Publications, 1984)
Calligraphy Today, revised edition, Heather Child (A & C Black/Taplinger, 1988)

Magazines
The Scribe, journal of the Society of Scribes and Illuminators
Calligraphy Review
Alphabet, the journal of the Friends of Calligraphy
Crafts, the magazine of the Crafts Council

'The Arrest of Oscar Wilde at the Cadogan Hotel', the poem by Sir John Betjeman which was used by Gerald Fleuss in the piece of work shown on the frontispiece of this book, appears by kind permission of John Murray (Publishers) Ltd.

Detail of a wall hanging by Ethna Gallacher.

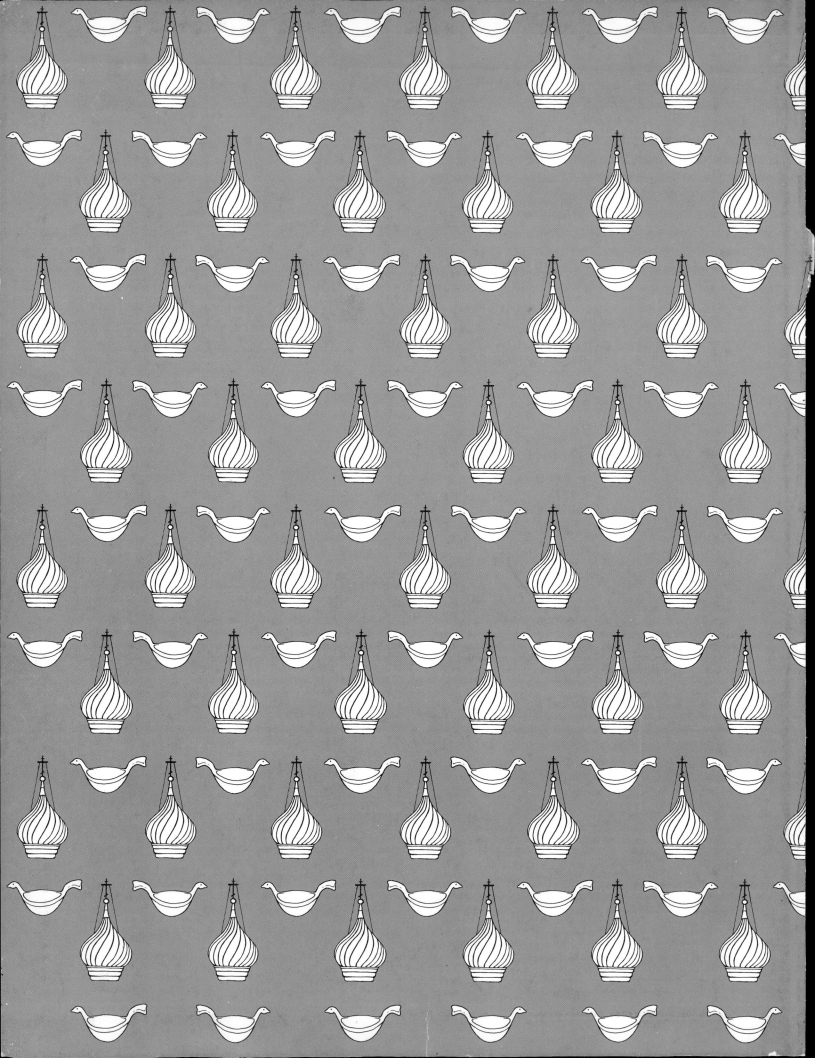